Great Teams of Pro Basketball

Exciting accounts of four of the greatest basketball teams of all time. Lou Sabin describes the heroics and the teamwork that brought each team to a championship. Included are the Minneapolis Lakers of 1952–53, the Philadelphia 76ers of 1966–67, the 1968–69 Boston Celtics and the 1969–70 New York Knicks.

Great Teams of Pro Basketball

By LOU SABIN

*I*llustrated with Photographs

RANDOM HOUSE
NEW YORK

To the memory of my father, Phillip Sabin,
and Jack Zanger, who got me into the business.

Copyright © 1971 by Random House, Inc.

All rights reserved under International and Pan-American Copyright Conventions. Published in the United States by Random House, Inc., New York, and simultaneously in Canada by Random House of Canada Limited, Toronto.

Trade Edition: ISBN: 0–394–82118–1
Library Edition: ISBN: 0–394–92118–6

Library of Congress Catalog Card Number: 72-158372

Manufactured in the United States of America

Contents

Introduction	vii
Minneapolis Lakers, 1952–53	3
Philadelphia 76ers, 1966–67	37
Boston Celtics, 1968–69	69
New York Knicks, 1969–70	99
Index	137

Introduction

What makes a basketball team great? Every season one team wins the championship in the National Basketball Association but the title doesn't necessarily make a team great. The teams described in the following pages were more than champions for a year—each one displayed a certain magical quality that made it a shining contributor to professional basketball.

The 1952–53 Minneapolis Lakers, with a starting lineup that boasted four of the great stars of that era, dominated pro basketball's early years as the New York Yankees had once dominated baseball. They towered head and shoulders above the league before pro basketball was a major sport and when it needed a giant to capture the public's interest. The Lakers helped basketball to survive so that it could become what it is today.

The Philadelphia 76er team of 1966–67 was testimony to one man's determination to lead a

INTRODUCTION

team to a championship. It was the best year in the fantastic career of Wilt Chamberlain, the NBA's all-time scoring machine, who sacrificed his tremendous scoring ability to become a team man, setting up scoring plays for others and battling for rebounds. His reward was the NBA championship and the best team record—68 wins and 13 losses—in league history.

The finest succession of basketball teams ever assembled was the Boston Celtics of the late 1950s and 1960s. The Celts won 11 championships in 13 years. The 1968–69 club, was the last team in the dynasty. In the regular season it finished only fourth in the Eastern Division, barely qualifying for the playoffs. Bill Russell and Sam Jones, who were so important in earlier championship seasons, were both past their prime as players. But this 1968–69 team deserves to be remembered with the greatest because it staged the most heroic comeback the sport has ever witnessed. The weary old Celtics proved that pride is one of the irreplaceable ingredients in the makeup of a champion.

The 1969–70 Knickerbockers contributed sheer basketball beauty as a total team, and showed just how effective defensive play can be in a league dominated by giant centers and high-scoring guards and forwards. The Knicks lacked a giant

INTRODUCTION

or a superstar but they proved that a perfectly organized team could go all the way—and set records in the process.

Even as you are reading this, other great teams are emerging. But they'll have to go a long way before they can justly claim a place alongside the teams described in this book.

I wish to express my appreciation for the help I received in the development of this book from the following: Bud Armstrong, Minneapolis *Tribune;* Bob Curran, Director of Public Relations, National Basketball Association; Al Silverman (Editor), Fred Katz (Managing Editor), and the other staff members of *Sport* magazine.

Photograph Credits:

Vernon J. Biever: 99, 100, 104, 107, 116, 121; Malcolm Emmons: 37, 38, 78, 83; George Kalinsky: 50, endpapers; United Press International: ii, vi, 3, 4, 9, 14, 18–19, 21, 29, 32–33, 47, 53, 57, 62, 65, 69, 70, 74–75, 88–89, 92, 95, 111, 126, 129, 133.

Cover photo: Vernon J. Biever

Great Teams of Pro Basketball

Minneapolis Lakers 1952-53

Big George Mikan, star of the Lakers, shoots a hook over Sweetwater Clifton of the New York Knicks.

John Kundla, coach of the Minneapolis Lakers, was worried. "We're in shape," he told reporters, "just dead tired." The 1952–53 basketball season was about to begin, but the Lakers had just played 14 games in 15 nights on an exhibition tour. The team had won the NBA championship the year before, and Kundla was confident that they would win again. "We expect to go all the way again," he said. "But there's been no time to rest in the last three weeks. Just look at those boys out there." He swept his hand in the direction of his players, who were warming up on the Minneapolis Auditorium basketball court. "They're really dragging."

Vern Mikkelsen, sweat streaming down his angular face, joined Kundla and the reporters. The broad-shouldered forward had been a powerful force in the 1951–52 Laker victory drive, averaging 15.3 points per game and 10.3 rebounds. Mikkelsen echoed his coach's complaint that everyone needed a few days' rest. To emphasize his point, he pointed to his knees and said, "I hurt from my toes right up to here. Everyone of us is aching somewhere."

The Minneapolis center, George Mikan, was more optimistic. He scoffed when the reporter suggested he might be slowing down. Mikan had led the NBA in scoring in 1949, 1950 and 1951, but he had missed the mark in 1952. "Me, slipping? At 28?" answered the muscular 240-pounder. "Not a bit. I'll admit I haven't been scoring in these exhibition contests, but you might say I'm simply pacing myself. We've got a long season coming up."

"We complained last year, too," Kundla chimed in. "But we were ready for that opening game." The Lakers had played a superb first game and had gone on to win their fourth world title in five years. This year they opened against the Celtics. "I just wish we didn't have to start this one against Boston," Kundla concluded.

The Celtics were not a league power, but they had improved rapidly under the shrewd, demanding coaching of Arnold "Red" Auerbach. The Boston squad boasted three of the league's finest shooters. Bob Cousy had a 19.8 scoring average in 1952 and was third in the league in total points.

MINNEAPOLIS LAKERS, 1952–53

Ed Macauley, the Celtic center, had finished just behind Cousy with five fewer points. And Bill Sharman was the NBA's free-throw leader and sixth highest scorer the previous year.

Cousy also had led the league in assists for 1952. His uncanny passing and brilliant playmaking had added new dimensions to the routine, stand-up style of basketball in the early 1950s. Only the Lakers' Slater Martin and the Knicks' Dick McGuire could stay with him when it came to ball-control and playmaking. The Celtics didn't have muscle men to match the Lakers' big three of Mikan, Mikkelsen and Jim Pollard, but Boston forwards Bob Brannum and Chuck Cooper weren't wallflowers when it came to battling for rebounds.

The Laker line-up that opened the 1952–53 season consisted of 6'10" Mikan at center, 6'5" Pollard and 6'7" Mikkelsen at the two forward posts, and, at the guard positions, 5'10" Slater Martin and veteran Pep Saul. Saul was substituting for the injured Whitey Skoog. These five took the floor against the Celtics as a staunchly partisan Minneapolis crowd of 5,359 chanted in the stands, "Get 'em, Lakers!" The ball went up for the opening tap-off and Mikan slapped it to Slater Martin.

Martin, who was called "Dugie" on the team,

dribbled deliberately toward the Laker basket. It was a familiar sight to Minneapolis followers. Dugie worked his way upcourt, giving Mikan time to set up near the basket, where he was most effective as a rebounder and deadly shooter. Pollard and Mikkelsen were also within jumping range of the backboard, ready to rebound or take a short feed from Mikan. Those three big men up front were the strength of the team which had dominated the league for five years.

Cousy stuck close to Martin, trying to cut off the pass that, he knew, would go floating into Mikan at any moment. Martin faked a pass once, twice, and finally forced Cousy to commit himself. Suddenly the ball flew over Cousy's head and dropped into Mikan's hands.

Only Boston's Ed Macauley was between Mikan and the basket. As the Laker center swung around for a hook shot, Easy Ed stopped the ball —but he also made contact with Mikan's hand. Mikan stepped to the foul line, made both foul shots and lumbered back on defense.

Defending against the smooth-moving Macauley proved a particularly tough job for Mikan that night. Taking brilliant passes from Cousy,

Slater Martin fights for possession of the ball with two opponents.

mixing hooks and drives and outside set shots with clever fakes, Macauley hit on 10 of 19 shots from the field and 17 out of 22 free throws. Neither Mikan nor his relief man, Lew Hitch, could contain Easy Ed, whose 37 points were high for the game. But apart from Cousy's 15 points, the total Celtic attack wasn't enough to counter the well-balanced Lakers. All five starters scored in double figures and Minneapolis defeated Boston 94–91.

In the second game of the season, against the Fort Wayne Pistons, overall team play resulted in a Laker victory, 81–69. And again, Pollard and Mikkelsen led the way with 18 and 16 points. But Kundla had reason to worry. Mikan, whose huge shoulders were expected to carry the weight of the Lakers' attack, had managed only six points against Fort Wayne. Mikan understood the importance of his role as a scorer. In an article he wrote for *Sport* magazine he said, "If you're a big, tall fellow who plays the pivot, your job is to score. Certainly that's my job—or at least the biggest part of it. Like every pivotman, I am so constantly near the basket that when I get the ball I have to be able to put it through the hoop. I know no one else on my team is going to be getting closer shots at the basket . . . In the pivot, I can take any shot that my teammates on the outside can take—and more besides.

MINNEAPOLIS LAKERS, 1952–53

"There's the routine over-the-head, two-hand set or the one-hand push—both taken while you're facing the basket. My height permits me to get off good jump shots too—shots that won't be blocked. While these are shots that almost any man on the floor can take, I still have a variety of shots unique to the pivot post. The old fallaway is tough to score with but it's important to have in your repertoire. When I'm being guarded closely, fading away from the basket gives me the room to arc the ball over my shoulder, over the outstretched hands of my defender and into the basket—I hope. Then there is the standard hook shot which a pivotman must be able to make regularly if he expects to get anywhere. It forces the defender to respect your offensive strength, and it sets up your best and most important shot—the layup. When your opponent starts watching for your hook shot, you can fake with a pivot and then drive around him for a layup. The fake-and-layup routine is the pivotman's most effective weapon. Naturally, it's the easiest shot to make and it puts you in position to rebound if the shot misses.

"With all this talk about scoring, it should not be forgotten that the pivotman has other jobs. He has to be able to execute passing assignments and he has to be in position to get the ball off the boards. In most games, when the pivot is having good success with his shots, the opposition tends to ignore his teammates and put a closer guard on him. That's when I concentrate on handing off or passing to players breaking around me."

But a pivotman unable to score regularly upsets the balance of the team built around his ability to do so—and after those first two games, Coach Kundla did, indeed, seem to have a major problem. Mikan's laughing remark, "Me, slipping? At 28?" was taking on serious meaning.

The third game of the season was against the Baltimore Bullets, a team that boasted a tall line-up. There were: 6'7" George Ratkovich, 6'7" Don Henriksen, 6'6" Don Barksdale and 6'4" Jim Baechtold. This meant that Mikan would be so busy fighting for rebounds that he might not have a chance to work out of his scoring slump. At least Whitey Skoog, the Lakers' regular guard, would be back in the line-up. His injury had healed and he was ready to play.

The question concerning Mikan's "slipping" at 28 was answered in the first quarter of play. He shut out Henriksen completely, keeping the Baltimore center away from the boards and boxing him in whenever he had the ball. And when the Lakers had the ball, it was Big Number 99 back in action, hooking, jump-shooting and dunking the ball. He controlled his territory with the ferocity of a furious bull and he also controlled the flow of the game by passing off every time the Bullets converged on him, zinging passes to Pollard and Mikkelsen on the sides, and to Skoog and Martin on the outside. With Big George back in form, the Lakers left the court at the end of the first quarter leading 18–12.

The Minneapolis massacre continued through the second quarter, and the Lakers led at halftime 41–27. By the end of the game, a happy, rejuvenated Mikan looked up at the scoreboard through his glasses and read: Minneapolis 97, Baltimore 75.

Now the Lakers really looked unstoppable. Not only was Number 99 back in the basket-making business, scoring 30 points, but the full Minneapolis balanced attack had been on display. Little Slater Martin had hit for 21 points (in addition to clamping down on the Bullets' best scorer), Pollard had collected 10 points, Mikkelsen 12, Skoog 12, and Harrison 12.

These individual totals and the final score seem small in comparison to today's scoring figures. The reason is that the 24-second rule had not yet been introduced to the professional game. Since a team did not have to shoot or give up the ball within any time limit, they could build a small lead and then control the ball for long periods.

The Lakers had demonstrated that a ball club

MINNEAPOLIS LAKERS, 1952–53

with a strong front line and a great scorer like Mikan had tremendous advantages. But the Lakers had another quality that contributed to their success—a willingness to share. Jim Pollard, for example, had been a college star at Stanford University before joining the Lakers. But he surrendered the top scoring role because he wanted to play for a team championship rather than a personal one. The Laker kind of sharing had its advantages, as Pollard pointed out. "Mikan's presence has really taken the heat off me," he said. "I couldn't stand the pressure of being the key man for 70 games in one season. Neither could he. It has been to the advantage of both of us that we wound up together. Playing with Mikan means you are on a winning team. A winner makes more money and enjoys his work more. And when you take a shot, it is always nice to know you have a fellow like Mikan under the basket, following up. It takes some of the responsibility off you if you miss."

Vern Mikkelsen was another college star who signed on with the Lakers knowing that he'd have to play a secondary role to Mikan. As a star at Hamline University, in nearby St. Paul, Mikkel-

Jim Pollard (17) and Vern Mikkelsen, two of the Lakers' Big Three, go up for a rebound.

sen had played only one position—center—and his best shot was a hook from the pivot. With Mikan solidly entrenched at center, Vern had to change his ways and become a forward. This meant learning new shots and techniques. "I studied the set-shot artists, such as Andy Phillip and Frank Brian," he said, "and I saw how they held both hands high, cradled the ball in them, and let her rip from overhead. They were small and I was big, so naturally, if I shot it from up there, a guy would have to guard me awful close to block the shot. That would also give me the chance to drive around him." He became a model forward.

Martin and Skoog could also score, but they knew their primary job on this team was playmaking and feeding. Playing on a team with Mikan, Pollard and Mikkelsen, they saw that it was sound basketball to feed rather than shoot.

The fourth game of the season for the Lakers was against the Philadelphia Warriors. The Warriors fielded a team that starred Neil Johnston, a center with a sweeping hook shot that was tough to stop. Johnston represented one of the major barriers to Mikan's quest to take the league's scoring title. Another Philadelphia basket-bombardier was Jumping Joe Fulks, who then held the record for most points scored in a pro basketball game, 63. There was also a family rivalry in the game, since George Mikan's brother, Ed, was in the Warrior line-up.

Game scoring honors went to Johnston, who netted 21 points, and Ed Mikan dropped in 17 for Philadelphia. But Slater Martin shackled Fulks, holding the great jump-shooter to only one foul point throughout the game. Contributing to the Lakers' 93–71 victory, their fourth straight, were double-figure performances by six of the Lakers. Big George led the way with 18, followed by Mikkelsen with 15, Pollard and Martin with 14 apiece, Pep Saul with 12, and Bob Harrison with 11. Even with Mikan back on the beam, balance was the byword.

That same night, the Rochester Royals posted *their* fourth straight victory. The two teams followed the same path in the next few games. Rochester lost to Milwaukee 78–75, and the Lakers were upset by the Syracuse Nationals 96–89. Both teams quickly got back on the right track. The Royals beat the New York Knicks 104–94, and the Lakers tripped Boston 101–92.

Then the Lakers traveled to New York to meet the team they had defeated in the championship playoffs the previous year, the New York Knick-

Backcourt man Whitey Skoog drives around a Philadelphia Warrior. ➤

erbockers. There was a good chance that the Knicks and Lakers would meet again in the playoffs to decide who would wear the crown for 1953. So both squads were anxious to test the other's strengths and weaknesses and to see whether their opponents had improved or added new talent or new plays. There was a renewal of personal battles, too. "Tricky" Dick McGuire, the passing marvel of the Knick backcourt, was sure to tangle with Dugie Martin in a great individual competition between two little men. Harry Gallatin, the Knicks' "Horse," was a master when it came to the bruising, elbowing, muscle-for-muscle warfare for rebounds. With Gallatin against the Laker forward wall would be the former Harlem Globetrotter battler, Nat "Sweetwater" Clifton. Shot for shot and shove for shove, the Knicks could hold their own against any team in the league.

After the game a sportswriter for the *Minneapolis Tribune* began his dispatch to the Laker fans: "The world champion Minneapolis Lakers slid unceremoniously out of a first-place tie in the Western Division of the National Basketball Association Thursday night by bowing to New York, 100–91, at Madison Square Garden."

The Knicks' Harry "the Horse" Gallatin (right) struggles with Vern Mikkelsen for the ball during the 1953 playoffs.

In fact, the Lakers were behind from the opening minutes. The Knicks were ahead by 14 at the half and never were threatened. The only bright spot for Laker fans was that George Mikan had another great night, scoring 32 points.

The Laker loss put their early-season mark at five wins and two losses. It was clear that they would not win another championship without opposition. It seemed possible that the kings of the hill might lose their position to one of the revenge-minded clubs they met along the way.

In their first meeting with Rochester, the Lakers learned that their strongest rivals meant business. The Royals conquered the Lakers 97–89. The Royals' center Arnie Risen scored 24 points and Bobby Wanzer's drives and outside set shots were good for 23. Now the Royals had a 7–1 won-lost mark, to the Lakers' 5–3. Suddenly the Lakers weren't the certain champs the experts had labeled them.

The Laker team could hardly be counted out, however. Coach Joe Lapchick of the Knicks reminded the sportswriters of what Big Number 99 had said about playing the professional way. Mikan had said, "There is a way in professional basketball, as well as in any other sport, to separate the men from the boys. Pressure is the big factor. The playoffs put more pressure on the individual players than anything else. You can have all the talent in the world, but if you're not interested in making the full use of that talent, victory is unlikely."

Coach Lapchick could hardly forget how George Mikan responded to the clutch situations. The Knicks had been victims of his pressure play more than once. So Lapchick and others who had followed Mikan's career knew that he well might launch a one-man crusade to lift the 5–3 Laker mark to a higher and higher winning percentage. And when he reached the playoffs, he seemed to be even bigger and stronger than in the regular season.

When Mikan heard about Lapchick's comments, he modestly reminded reporters that no one man could make a team a winner. His reminder echoed his comments of the season before when, in January of 1952, he had slammed 61 points through the nets in one game against Rochester. "There was a lot of fuss about my 61 points," the Laker center said, "99 percent of it about me. Jim Pollard, Dugie Martin and the rest of the boys hardly got a mention. Yet if it hadn't been for them, I couldn't have gotten 21 points. All you have to do on this club is stand around and wait for somebody to throw you the ball."

In the next six games Big George "stood

around," as he modestly put it. When the ball magically appeared in his hands, it usually sailed magically into the basket. Minneapolis won the next six in a row, overtaking the Royals in the race for first place. George sometimes took charge of the scoring and sometimes devoted his energies to passing to whichever Laker had his shooting eye. Depending on which team he faced—and which center—George applied his talents accordingly. In addition to rebounds and assists, Mikan scored 14, 31, 35, 17, 9 and 21 points. Including his 32 points in the loss against Rochester, he had a seven-game total of 159 points, or close to 23 points per game. His performance would be impressive today, but in those days of lower scores it was fantastic.

The Rochester Royals brought the Lakers down to earth again with an 83–71 streak-stopper. But the Lakers weren't stopped for long. They got moving again in the next game, against Philadelphia, winning 91–66. Mikan rolled in 23 points in 32 minutes of play. They repeated in their next contest, against Baltimore, posting another top-heavy win of 89–67. Boston's Celtics fell under the Laker juggernaut next, followed by the Knicks for two in a row. Minneapolis had won 5 in a row and 11 of their last 12. Mikan was averaging 19 points per game for the season.

MINNEAPOLIS LAKERS, 1952–53

It took an injury to Jim Pollard to stop the Lakers again. With the big forward sitting out the next game, not even Mikan's 25-point performance could avoid an 81–76 loss to the fourth-place Indianapolis Olympians. The Lakers came back to nip the Syracuse Nationals 82–79, with Vern Mikkelsen playing hero on 31 points. Their next game was against the second-place Rochester Royals, who trailed the Lakers by two games. This time Minneapolis smothered Rochester 95–77, avenging their two earlier losses to the challengers.

The Lakers still had their lead at midseason when the league paused for the All-Star game on January 13. Three Lakers had been selected to the Western Division team and Coach Kundla directed the squad. Mikan and Mikkelsen started the game and Slater Martin saw action later. The headline story once more was George Mikan. Number 99 bucketed 22 points and snared 16 rebounds in 40 minutes of playing time. The West beat the Eastern Division team 79–75 and Mikan was voted the Most Valuable Player award.

Then Big George really poured it on in the Lakers' next league game. His victims were the Baltimore Bullets, who were helpless to stop the Mikan onslaught of 46 points and 28 rebounds. The Bullets had an attack of their own, however, and the Lakers just pulled out a 112–104 victory in double overtime.

The win put the Minneapolis season record at 29 wins and 9 losses, which meant a $3\frac{1}{2}$-game edge over the Rochester Royals. The race was closer in the Eastern Division, where Syracuse, Boston and New York were trading the lead almost on a day-to-day basis.

By the middle of March the dust had settled in both divisions. The Knicks had clinched first place in the East, having come on hard and fast as the season grew shorter and shorter. And the Lakers wrapped up the Western title with a convincing 89–77 conquest of the second-place Rochester Royals. It was a typical Laker demonstration, with Jim Pollard scoring 18 points, Slater Martin setting up plays and feeding the ball to the big three, and Mikan doing business as usual—rebounds aplenty, rugged boardwork and 28 points.

The regular season ended with Minneapolis owning a record of 48 wins and 22 losses. The Knicks finished at 47–23. If the two teams met in the finals, the Lakers would have the first game at home because their season record was one game better.

The Lakers welcomed the few days of rest before the playoffs began. George Mikan could use the time to recover from the bruises acquired in the constant bang-and-shove battles under the boards and from the disappointment of losing the scoring title to Neil Johnston. George had scored 1,442 points for a 20.6 per-game mark; Johnston had notched 1,564 points for a 22.3 per-game mark. In some ways it didn't seem fair: Johnston's Philadelphia team had finished dead last in the East, with an abysmal record of 12 wins and 57 losses. Mikan's consolation was that he had captured the rebound title from Johnston, grabbing 1,007 caroms to Johnston's 976. Vern Mikkelsen scored 1,047 points for a 15-point average, and Jim Pollard had chipped in with 859 points or 13 points per game. Between them, the Big Three in Minneapolis had averaged nearly 50 points.

In the Eastern playoff semifinals, the Knicks beat Baltimore two straight in the best-of-three series. Then they took Boston three games to one in their best-of-five series. In the West, Minneapolis stopped Indianapolis in two straight, 85–69 and 81–79. Then they overcame a surprising Fort Wayne team in the fifth and deciding game, 74–58. Thus the Lakers and the Knicks met in the championship series for the second year in a row.

Minneapolis was favored to beat New York in the best-of-seven series. But taking on the Lakers didn't worry the Knicks' coach Joe Lapchick. "We know we're going against the champions,"

Lapchick said before the first game, "but I know what my boys can do. I've seen them come through enough times this year. They'll never quit."

Lapchick did have problems, however. One of his best shooters, Max Zaslofsky, was out with a broken hand, and guard Al McGuire had suffered a broken jaw, which had been wired together. He would see limited action at best. This left New York with Nat Clifton, Carl Braun, Vince Boryla, Harry Gallatin, Ernie Vanderweghe, Dick McGuire and Connie Simmons. The Lakers were at full strength. Coach Kundla's first five consisted of Mikan, Pollard, Mikkelsen, Martin, and Bob Harrison, who had worked his way into the starting line-up. The Laker bench held guards Whitey Skoog and Pep Saul, forwards Jim Holstein and Dick Schnittker and reserve center Lew Hitch.

True to Lapchick's words, his Knicks "came through" in the first game. Although Mikan led all scorers with 25 points, New York, on the strength of a balanced scoring attack, downed the Lakers 96–88.

The second game, also on Minneapolis' home court, wasn't decided until late in the fourth quar-

Mikan tries to drive between two Knicks during the fourth playoff game but gets his arm hooked by Connie Simmons.

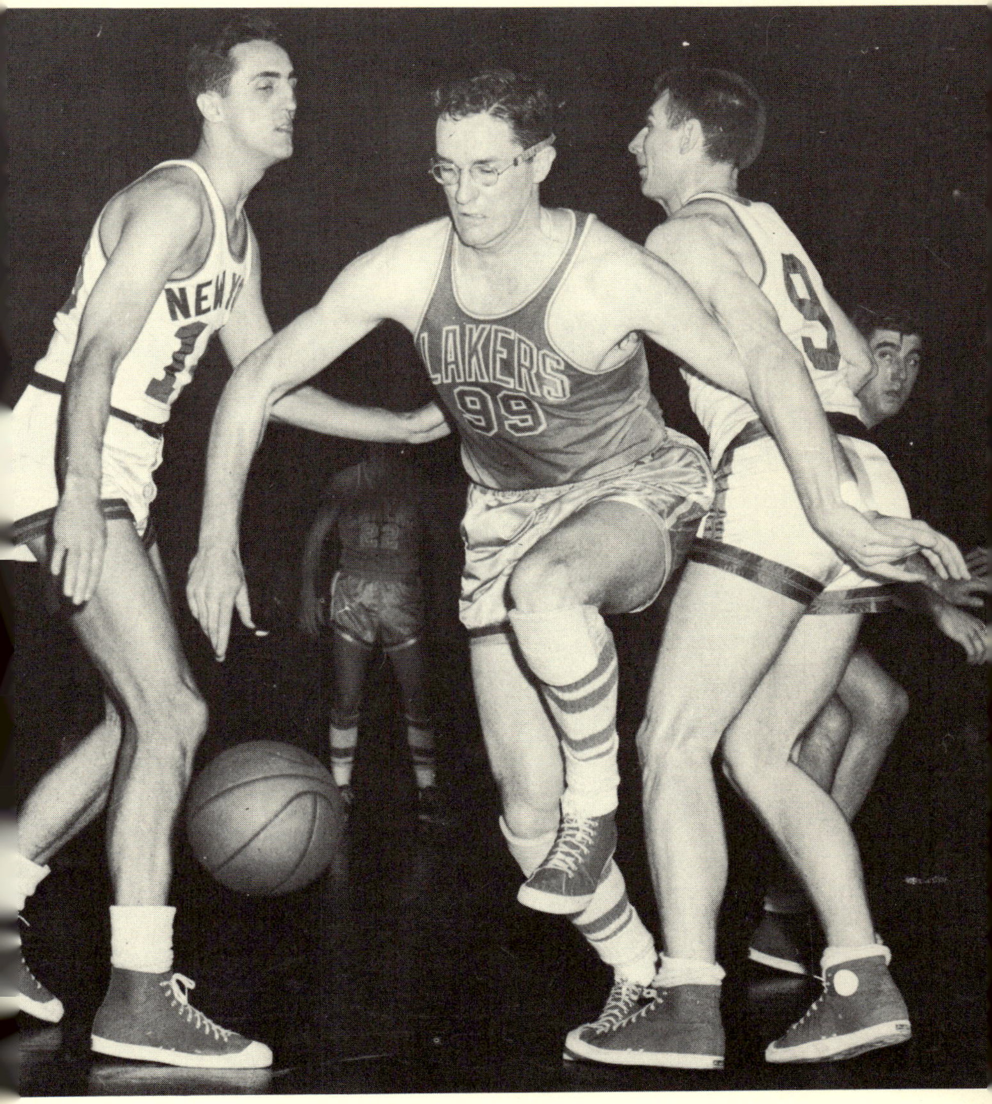
NEW
LAKERS
99

ter. In the closing minutes Mikan blocked Connie Simmons' crucial hook shot, and Pollard stopped Carl Braun's drive to the basket in the last minute of play. Then clutch shots by Pollard and Holstein gave the Lakers a narrow 73–71 win. Mikan again was high scorer, with 18.

The pre-finals predictions of a Minneapolis runaway sounded silly at this point in the series. On their own court, the Lakers could do no better than split two games with the Knicks, and the game they did win was a squeaker. Now the action was shifting to Knick territory for the next three games. The New York players were confident of taking the crown away from Minneapolis. Knick guard Carl Braun remarked, "Minneapolis is a nice town to play in. Too bad we won't be back." To which New York forward Ernie Vanderweghe added, "We'll be back—next year."

Mikan answered for all the Lakers when he stated, "It's a seven-game series. We'll get them."

That's precisely what Mikan and Company did. The third game saw Skoog and Harrison handcuff Venderweghe every time he tried to ignite a New York rally. At the same time Slater Martin shadowed Dick McGuire's every move, restricting the flashy Knick to just two points. Meanwhile, Mikan and Pollard took charge of

MINNEAPOLIS LAKERS, 1952–53

the scoring work, Big George clicking for 20 points, Pollard for 19. And the Lakers went one up in the series with a 90–75 victory.

Game four developed into a down-to-the-wire thriller. Vanderweghe and McGuire were throttled again, but Connie Simmons' pivot play and Carl Braun's outside shooting countered the attack mounted by Mikan, with support from Pollard and Mikkelsen. At first it looked as if Minneapolis was in total command, taking a 21–16 lead after the first quarter. Mikan was playing like Superman, scoring 18 of the Lakers' 21 points.

But New York kept on counterattacking and, with 2:29 left in the game, a Vanderweghe bucket tied the score at 62 apiece. Then the teams started trading fouls, and the Lakers' prospects looked glum when Mikan fouled out, leaving the game with the score tied at 65–65. As if to prove that Mikan wasn't the whole Laker offense, Whitey Skoog immediately raced downcourt, slanted his muscular body through a thicket of Knicks and whipped in a two-pointer. Skoog's basket was followed by foul shots by Pollard and Holstein, and the Lakers suddenly led by four. The Knicks made a desperate rush in the waning seconds, but fell short as the Lakers notched their third win, 71–69. Mikan's 27 points was the big story, but it

The victorious Lakers pose for a celebration picture in the dressing room after winning the NBA championship. Coach Kundla and Slater Martin are at front center with George Mikan between them.

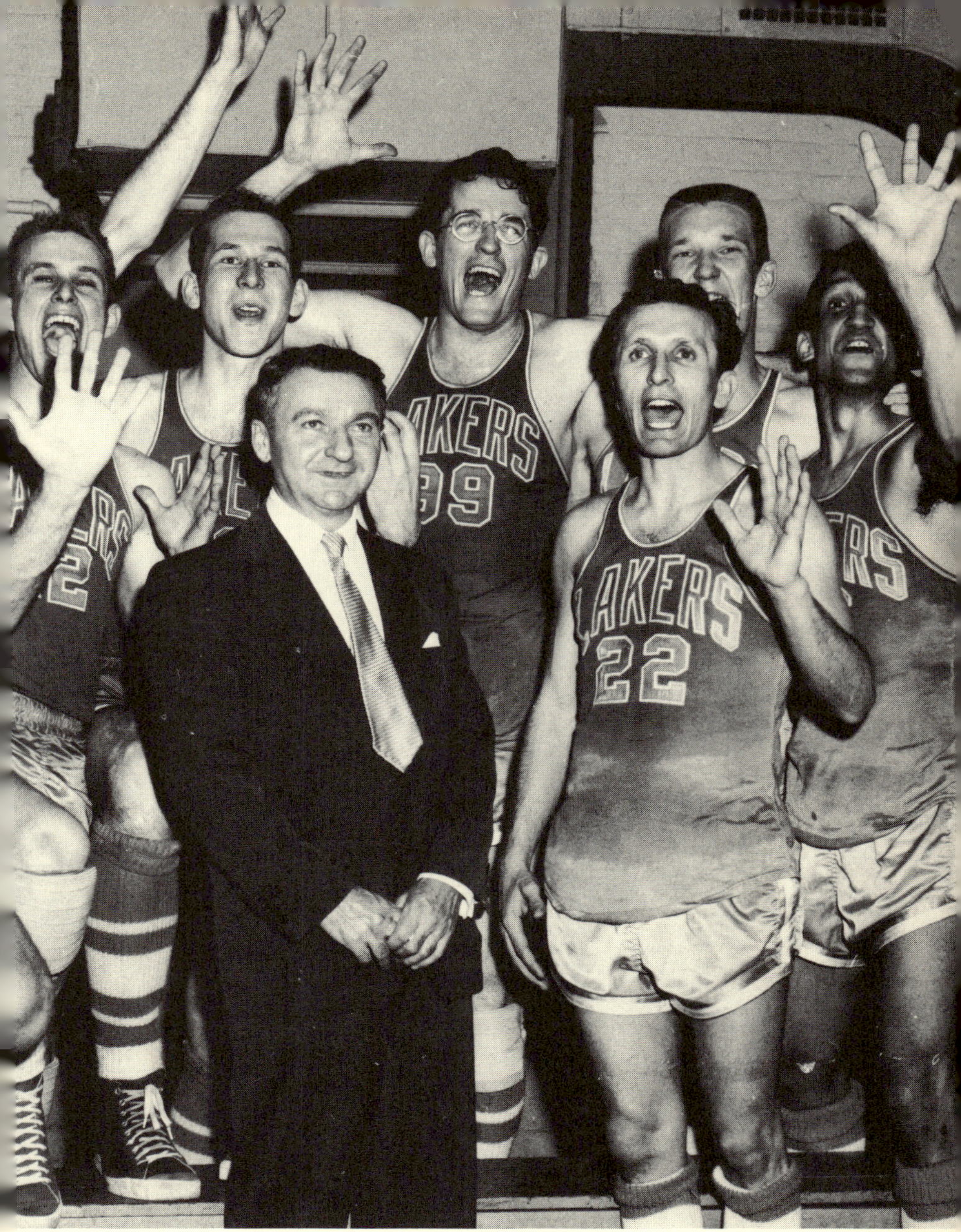
LAKERS
99
LAKERS
22

was a unified Minneapolis effort that made the difference.

In the fifth game the Knicks and Lakers put on another show that featured sharp, hard basketball and rough play. In the third period there was even a fight between Bob Harrison and Vince Boryla. The Harrison-Boryla battle ended in a draw, but the game ended with another championship for Minneapolis as the Lakers won 91–84.

The Knicks had boasted that they wouldn't be back in Minneapolis that season—and they were right. But the script had been reversed and the Lakers swept the three games in New York instead of the Knicks. Big George Mikan was delighted by what he called "a team affair." "This title is the sweetest of any of the five we have won in the last six years," he concluded.

The Lakers had again asserted their superiority over all challengers. And in doing so, they had added still another scalp to the championship belt they wore as the first dynasty in the history of professional basketball.

Minneapolis Lakers, 1952-53

Statistics

Regular season:
Team record: Won 48, lost 22. Finished first in Western Division.
Individual leaders:

	Games	Points	Points per Game	Rebounds	Assists
Mikan	70	1,442	20.6	1,007	201
Mikkelsen	70	1,047	15.0	654	148
Pollard	66	859	13.0	452	231

Playoff record:
First round, vs. Indianapolis (best 2 out of 3)
    MINNEAPOLIS   85   Indianapolis   69
    MINNEAPOLIS   81   Indianapolis   79
Second round, vs. Fort Wayne (best 3 out of 5)
    MINNEAPOLIS   83   Fort Wayne   73
    MINNEAPOLIS   82   Fort Wayne   75
    Minneapolis   95   FORT WAYNE   98
    Minneapolis   82   FORT WAYNE   85
    MINNEAPOLIS   74   Fort Wayne   58
Championship round, vs. New York (best 4 out of 7)
    Minneapolis   88   NEW YORK   96
    MINNEAPOLIS   73   New York   71
    MINNEAPOLIS   90   New York   75
    MINNEAPOLIS   71   New York   69
    MINNEAPOLIS   91   New York   84

Philadelphia 76ers 1966-67

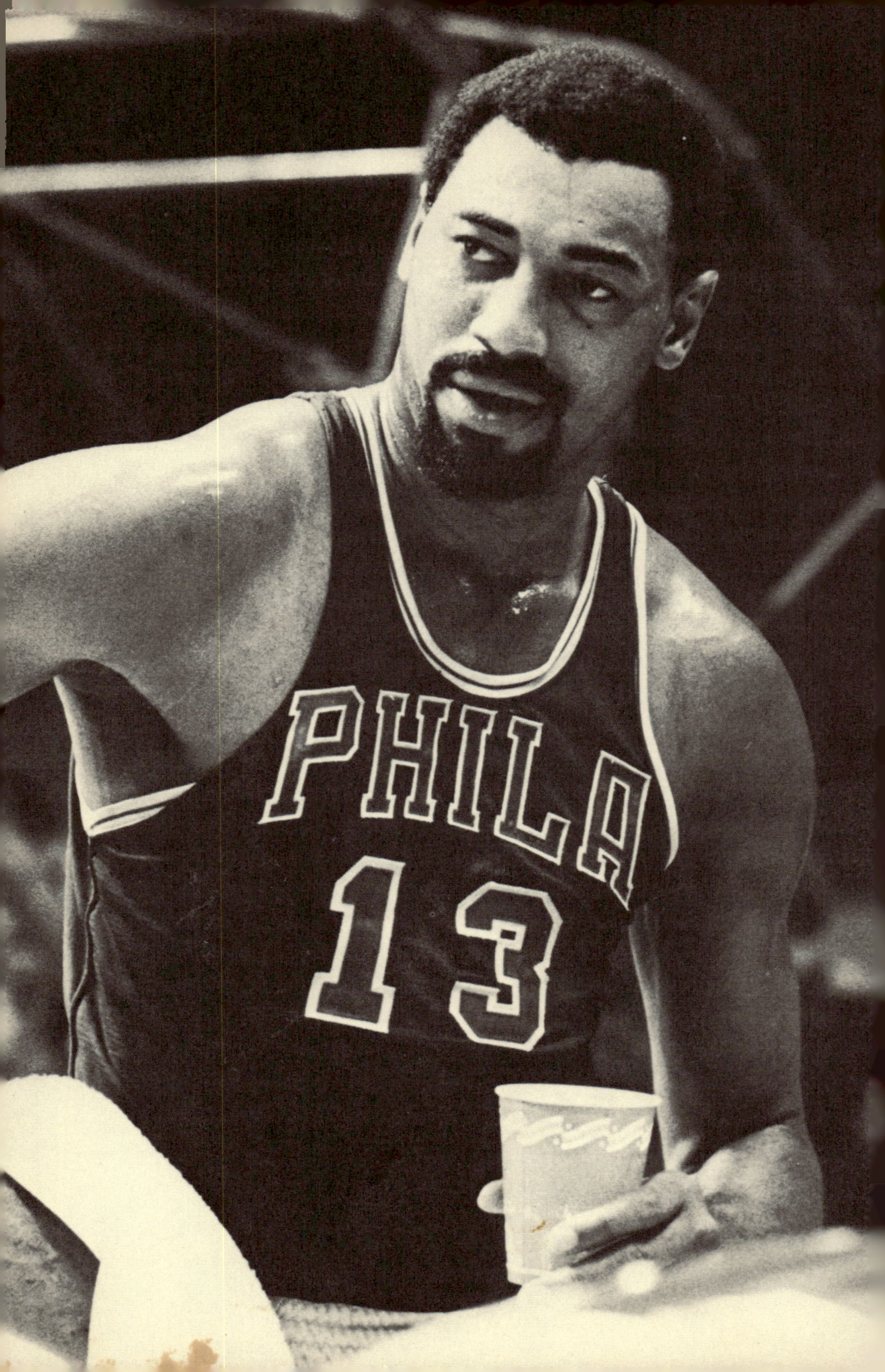
PHILA
13

The 76ers' big center, Wilt Chamberlain.

As a young man, Wilt Chamberlain was the super-everything. He was a fine quarter-miler whose long, powerful legs carried him in galloping strides around a track in excellent competitive times. He was a huge, powerhouse of a man who might have become a champion prize fighter or wrestler. He was tall and sure-handed and might have become a great receiver for some lucky professional football team. But Wilt showed his greatest talent on the basketball court. Who could doubt, after witnessing his play at Philadelphia's Overbrook High and at the University of Kansas, that Wilt Chamberlain could make a champion of any pro basketball team? Long before Wilt entered the pros, fans were saying that he and any four midgets would make mincemeat of the NBA.

But this giant of a man—standing 7'1" and weighing 275 pounds—entered his eighth season in the NBA as the tallest, heaviest question mark in the history of professional basketball. The question was, Why hadn't Wilt ever led an NBA team to a title? Even his college team, Kansas, had not won a championship with him. Wilt had once scored 100 points in an NBA game, a record that may never be approached. In 1961–62, he had *averaged* 50.4 points per game. But since his high school days none of the teams he played on had ever been a champion.

At the beginning of the 1966–67 season, sportswriters approached Chamberlain's boss, Alex Hannum. Hannum had recently become coach of Wilt's Philadelphia 76ers. But he was no stranger to Wilt, who had played two years for him in San Francisco. When the writers asked about Chamberlain's losing ways, Hannum said Wilt had assured him that he wanted desperately to be a winner. "Remember," Hannum said, "Wilt became an all-around player for me in 1963. That's what he's going to be this year, too. My idea is that in order to have a better team effort, Wilt must do more than just score. The trouble seems to be that since high school, he has been trained to receive the ball, pivot and shoot. He was told that the best way he could help his club was to score. But I've impressed on him that if we are to win, we must develop a more varied attack instead of just feeding him and letting him shoot."

PHILADELPHIA 76ERS, 1966–67

Hannum was convinced that no single player, even a Chamberlain, could do it all by himself. But with a cooperative Chamberlain, the 76ers had the potential to blast the league apart. To prove his point, Hannum pointed out how talented the rest of the team was.

First there was Hal Greer, one of the best guards in the game. He was fast. "I must be fast," Greer said, "always, always quick. The day I slow down I'm finished." And he was a constant scoring threat. Said his former coach, Dolph Schayes, "Hal has the finest middle-distance shot in the game. From 15 to 18 feet, Hal is more deadly than Oscar Robertson." At 6'2", 175 pounds, Greer was agile, strong and not prone to injury. An eight-year veteran of NBA play, he could be counted on to average 20 points a game and contribute steadily in assists.

Billy Cunningham was already well-known as a great "sixth man," able to come off the bench and pour in points. A 6'6", 220-pound forward, he could outleap and out-rebound opposing forwards with remarkable ease. He had learned his basketball on the playgrounds of Brooklyn, New York, and his skills included swiftness, aggressiveness and a weird assortment of shots. "You really can't stop Cunningham," said one opponent after a typical game for Billy. "The funny thing is, I

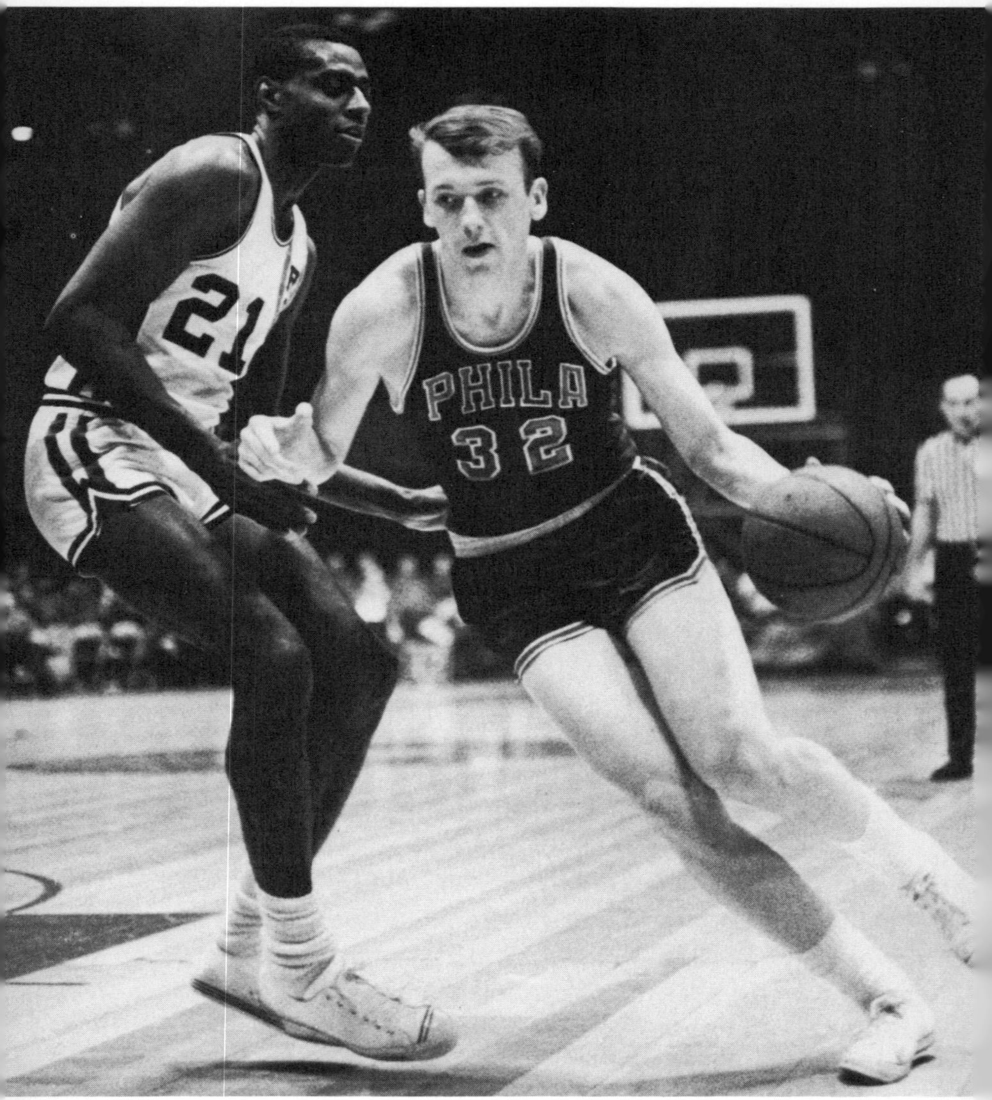
21
PHILA
32

PHILADELPHIA 76ERS, 1966–67

don't think he can make as many of his shots when nobody's on him. He needs contact. And when he gets it, it's like he's playing schoolyard ball again. His eyes light up. He really likes to go down the middle or across it, hanging up there and making shots under his arm and every which way." Cunningham was already an established star, although the previous year had been his rookie season. Hannum was considering giving him a starting role instead of keeping him on the bench as a supersub.

Chet Walker was back for his fifth season as a pro forward. Like Cunningham, the 6'6", 220-pounder was a trifle short to play up front, but that didn't stop him from snaring rebounds and hitting for a reliable 15-points-per-game average. He was also agile, a quality that Hannum was relying on to make the 76ers a smooth-running machine.

Lucious Jackson, also a forward, put his 6'9", 240-pound frame to good use as a rebounder. With Jackson, Cunningham and Walker, Philadelphia had as good a trio of forwards as any in the league.

Keeping Greer company in the backcourt were

Billy Cunningham often played "sixth man" for the 76ers, coming in to lift the team's performance in crucial moments.

a perfect pair of guards. One was Wally Jones, in his third season as a pro. Not only could the 6'2", 180-pound Jones hit for points, set up plays and make his share of assists, he could help keep the team loose through a long, tense season with his sense of humor, and his easygoing ways. As Hannum said, "Every team should have a Wally Jones."

The other guard was Larry Costello, who had announced his retirement after the previous season but had decided to rejoin the team now that Hannum was the coach. The 6'1", solidly built Costello brought with him excellent defensive talents, and his long experience in the league gave him the ability to take charge of the team on the court. Costello probably "smelled a championship," as one sportswriter remarked.

The substitutes behind these men added reliability and depth. Dave Gambee was another 6'6" forward who had been a pro for eight years and could be called on to battle for rebounds and play solid defense. And Philadelphia's No. 1 draft choice, Matt Guokas, showed promise of quickly becoming another fine playmaker in the backcourt. The other rookie was Bill Melchionni, also a good prospect.

Some observers still doubted that a Chamberlain-led team would win the championship. But

PHILADELPHIA 76ERS, 1966–67

this 76er squad had convinced many that the reign of the Boston Celtics, who had won the title eight years in a row, was about to end.

Philadelphia began to convince the doubters shortly after the season got under way. The 76ers, who had finished the previous year's regular season with 11 straight victories, picked up where they left off. With the "new" Wilt playing an all-around game, the 76ers won their first seven games, giving them an 18-game win streak over two seasons. Although this tied the NBA record of 18 victories in a row, the league record keepers put an asterisk next to the mark because the 18 consecutive wins had not come in a single season.

The 18th win was a 134–129 fourth-quarter win over the San Francisco Warriors. Philadelphia's balanced attack made the difference. Chamberlain had 30 points, Chet Walker had 30, and Hal Greer had 27. Warrior star Rick Barry scored 46, but his team lost. His performance seemed to support Hannum's argument that no single player could make a team a consistent winner.

The season had begun in late October and by December 11 the picture was pretty clear. The Boston Celtics had a 21–5 record, for a stunning .808 winning percentage. But the 76ers had an incredible 26–3 record for an .897 percentage.

The 76ers' success story had three parts. The

first part was Coach Hannum's accomplishment in making the club play as a team rather than a collection of individual stars. The second part was the balance the team possessed. This showed in the scoring columns: Chamberlain was averaging 24.8 points a game, Hal Greer 22, Chet Walker 20, and Billy Cunningham 17. The third part of the story was Big Wilt. He was averaging fewer than 14 shots a game, but connecting on 70 percent of them. He was also averaging 23.5 rebounds and seven assists per game.

By December 28, the 76ers had won five more games, giving them a 31–3 record. They seemed to get better with each game. Chamberlain obviously enjoyed being the king of rebounds, and seeing that his assists were paying off in points for the team. The entire team—and the Philadelphia fans—were amazed at the ease with which the victories were accomplished. Some games were so lopsided that hometown fans sometimes chanted, "Break up the 76ers!" as they watched their team at Philadelphia's new sports arena, The Spectrum.

Some 76er boosters were calling on Chamberlain to pass off less and shoot more. But Hannum

Wilt Chamberlain uses all his height, weight and muscle to take a rebound from San Francisco's Nate Thurmond.

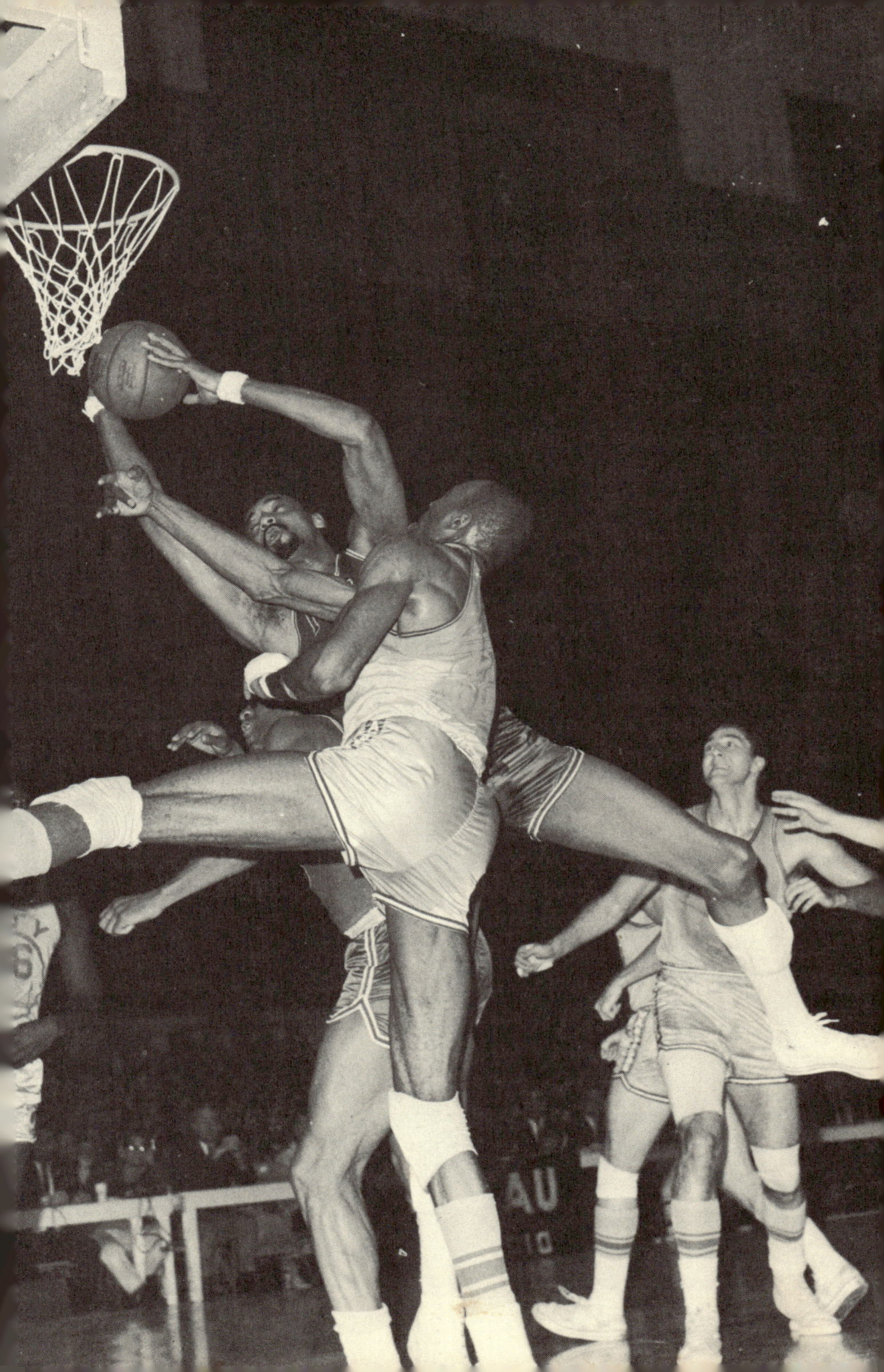

wasn't about to allow his team to give up their winning combination. Instead of permitting anyone to free-lance, he pushed the players to play even tighter defense, to hustle more and to imagine that the score was tied when they had a 20-point lead.

"The fellows tell me that last year if they built up a big lead, they'd relax and often blow the lead," Hannum explained. "That's why I want this team to keep going. I'm always concerned about them losing momentum. These other teams are all professional teams and if you start messing around with a ten-point lead, it doesn't take much to lose it."

A game in early January, against the New York Knickerbockers, showed just how tough NBA opposition could be—and how the 76ers were ready to rise to the challenge. The game was a see-saw battle well into the fourth quarter, featuring model team play and accurate shooting on both sides. Billy Cunningham, for one, was doing his wildest, weirdest best, shooting and scoring from all angles and making all kinds of dazzling moves. He scored 36 points. Meanwhile, Chamberlain was battling Knick centers Willis Reed and Walt Bellamy, dominating them off the boards at both ends of the floor. In addition, he was hitting the open man with pass after pass.

PHILADELPHIA 76ERS, 1966–67

The Knickerbockers were playing at their very best. Despite the strength of the 76er machine, the score was 122–111 in New York's favor with less than six minutes left. Philly caught up, but then the Knicks got some sharp outside shooting by Howard Komives and some give-and-go breakaways featuring Komives and Dick Barnett. With less than a minute left, the Knicks led 133–128.

That should have wrapped it up for the New Yorkers. But with 45 seconds between the 76ers and defeat, Chamberlain scored on a slamming bucket against the defensive try of Walt Bellamy, cutting the margin to three points. A moment later, Bellamy took a pass in the pivot and went up for a shot. But he met Chamberlain on the way up and missed the shot. Wilt snared the rebound and shoveled it to Chet Walker, who set up a 76er fast break. Hal Greer got the ball downcourt and drove for the basket. Suddenly he put on the brakes about 12 feet out and scored a one-hander. The shot was good for two points and Komives fouled him in the act of shooting. Greer made the foul shot and the 76ers had tied the game with 19 seconds remaining.

Neither team scored in the remaining seconds. But in the overtime period it was no contest. The 76ers had broken the Knicks' morale. The 76ers outscored the Knicks 15–9 in overtime and won

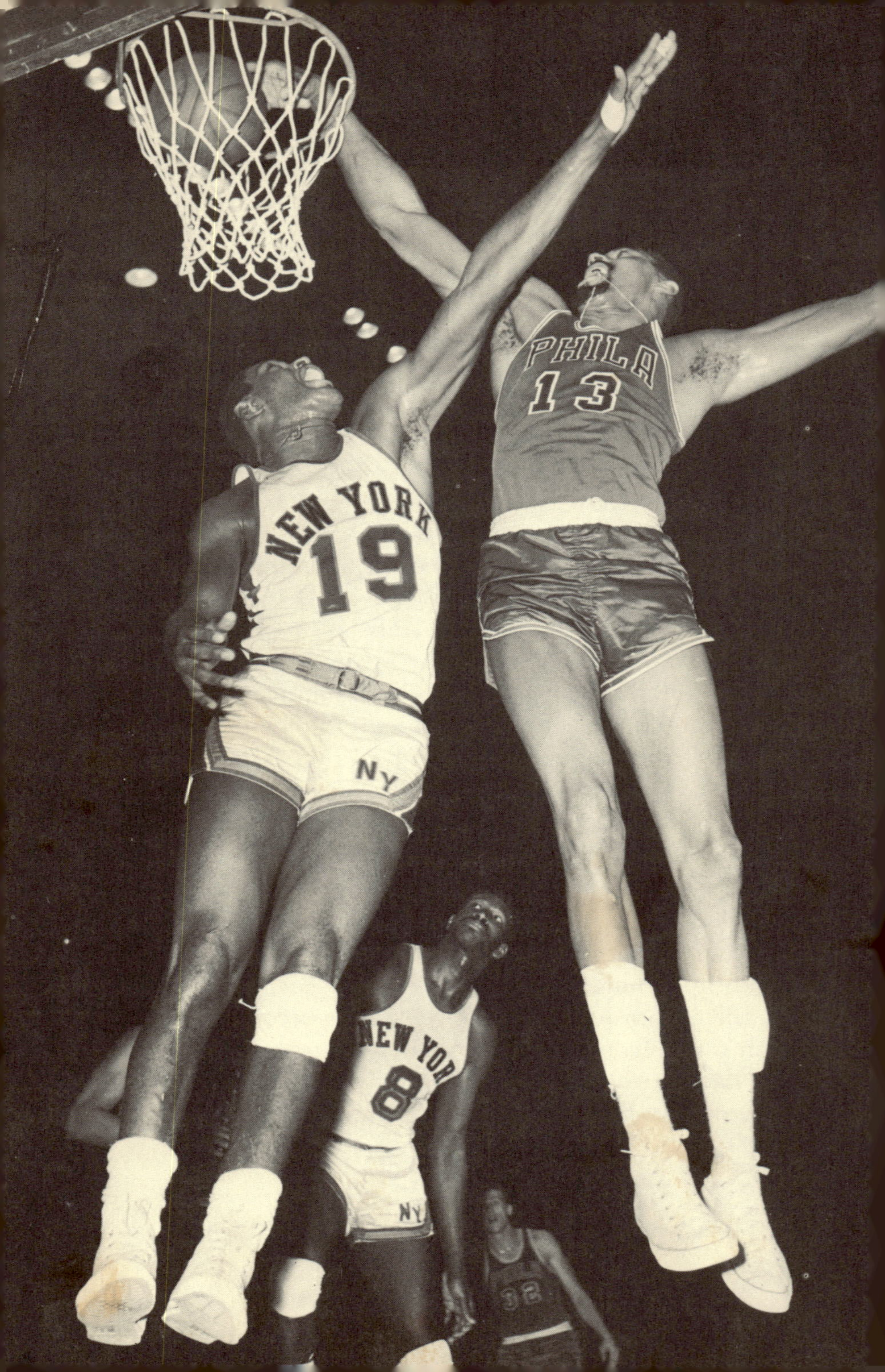

PHILA
13
NEW YORK
19
NY
NEW YORK
8
NY

PHILADELPHIA 76ERS, 1966–67

148–142. Hannum's squad had notched its 36th win in 39 games, and Chamberlain's personal contribution was 35 points, 33 rebounds. Thirteen of his rebounds came during the 76ers' torrid fourth-quarter comeback.

In the words of Leonard Koppett, viewing the game from the press box at Madison Square Garden: "The Knicks played the best basketball that this group of Knick players has played . . . it may have been the best basketball played by a Knick team. But it wasn't good enough to win because the 76ers, who are without much argument the most powerful basketball team, physically, ever put together, also played near the top of their game."

One rival NBA player expressed the feelings of other teams in the NBA: "You get one shot against that team and you better hope the ball goes in the basket, because if it doesn't, either Chamberlain or Jackson or Walker is going to get the rebound. Going after rebounds against them is like battling a buzz saw."

Coach Hannum continued to receive much of the credit for Philadelphia's success. But he gave most of the credit to his players. "I like to think

Big Wilt stuffs the ball into the basket against the Knicks' Willis Reed.

I've added something," he said, "but it hasn't been very much. I keep them enthusiastic about winning, to keep hustling and trying all the time. That's the essence of a coach's job. The technical aspects of basketball can be gotten from a textbook—it's the coach's business to make sure they're in the proper frame of mind."

Hannum also described the way Wilt Chamberlain was used on the team. "Wilt is putting more emphasis on defense. He realizes he's playing with the best team he's ever had and he knows it doesn't have to depend on him so much for scoring. Greer, Cunningham and Walker have been scoring well, so why should Wilt stop doing what he's been doing?

"Of course, before we win the title there will be phases in critical games where we are going to need heavy scoring from him, and that's when we'll look for him to get us points. I try to get the players to know who has the hot hand and to milk it. When no one has the hot hand, we go to Wilt. This is a balanced team, and that's what is behind our success. Basketball is a team game, the finest team game ever devised. You have to work together to win."

Philadelphia coach Alex Hannum jumps with excitement in the closing moments of a close game.

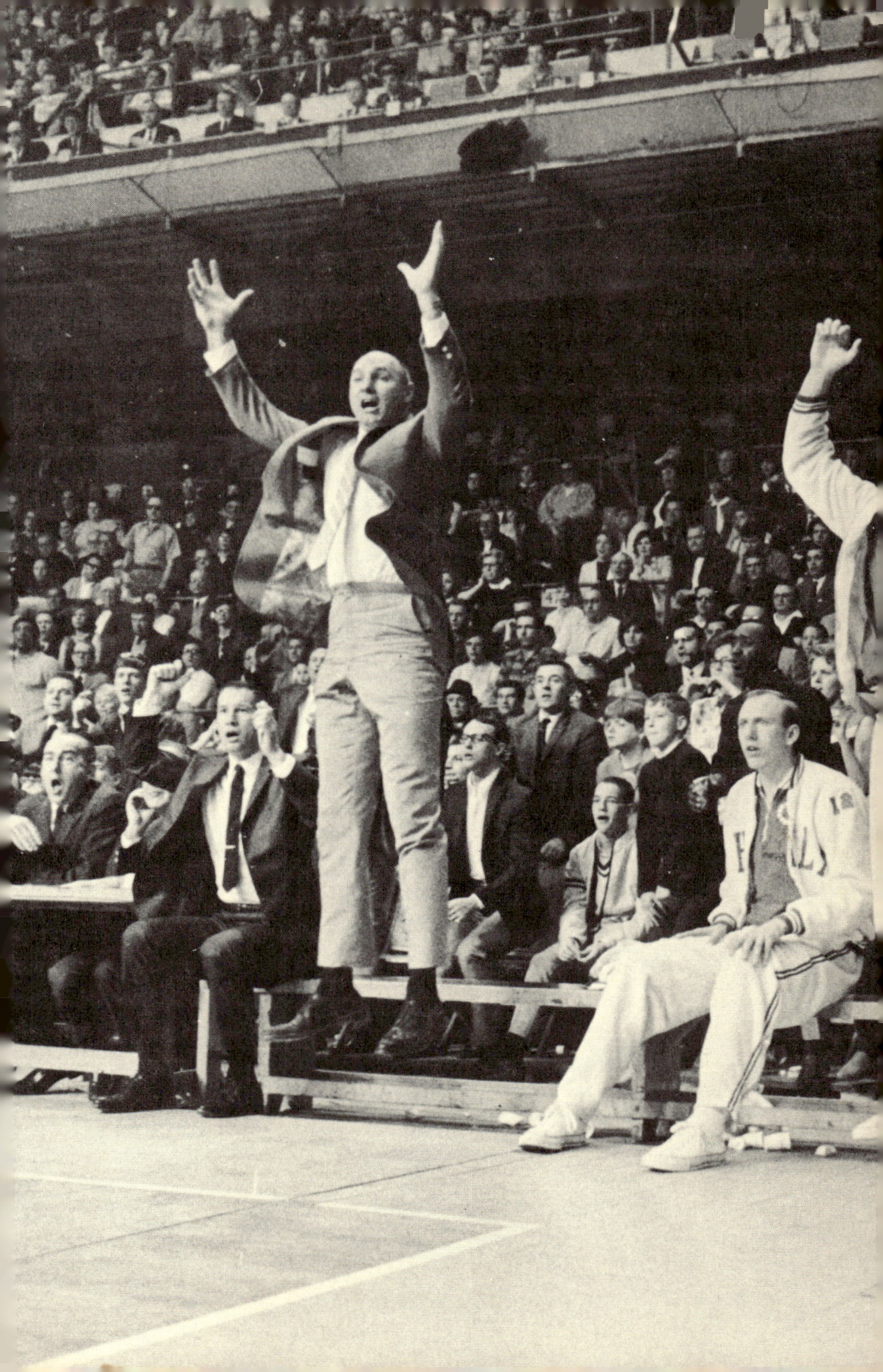

Philadelphia's record in mid-January was 39–3, the best midseason mark ever compiled in the NBA. But the season was not over. The Boston Celtics, with the fantastic Bill Russell, had compiled a 32–7 record to that point in the season, including two wins over Philadelphia.

Russell and Company represented the major threat to the 76ers in the Eastern Division. After the regular season, the 76ers would have to meet the Celtics and beat them in the divisional playoffs, too, if they were to have a chance at the NBA crown. Then the 76ers would have to meet the Western Division winners, probably San Francisco, in the championship series. The Warriors had the high-scoring Rick Barry and the mighty center work of Nate Thurmond, plus a well-rounded team. Hannum would have to keep his team rolling right along or it could falter and make its amazing won-lost record an embarrassment.

One of Hannum's difficulties was something every winning coach faces. It is always difficult for a team to "get up" for every game. But it is especially hard for a team that enjoys a commanding lead over all other competitors. And so, the 76ers fell prey to mild slumps, to weariness from the demanding travel schedule, and to occasional overconfidence. Nevertheless, on March 19, Philadel-

PHILADELPHIA 76ERS, 1966–67

phia wrapped up the regular 1966–67 season by notching a 132–129 win over the Baltimore Bullets for their 68th victory of the campaign. Combined with only 13 losses, the pros from the City of Brotherly Love posted a winning percentage of .840, the highest in the history of the NBA.

In that last contest, Chamberlain showed he was ready for the playoffs by scoring 37 points. He scored on 16 of 16 shots from the field and 5 for 7 from the free-throw line (a major accomplishment, since he was a notoriously poor foul-shooter). In addition, he swept away 30 rebounds against Baltimore's powerful center, Gus Johnson.

The Celtics finished a full eight games behind the 76ers in the Eastern Division. But the experts still gave them a good chance against the 76ers in the playoff. Boston had pride, playoff experience, and an amazing playoff record—eight championships in the last eight years.

Still, Philadelphia had some advantages. Of course, their record showed that they had played better during the regular season. In addition, their record would give them a home-court advantage in the crucial games of the playoff series. The team respected the Celtics but they remained confident. Hal Greer said, "You just naturally play harder against your best opposition. Boston's defense, you know, is their strong point. That's why we're going to have to play better. But I'm certain that when we're playing ball as a team, we're unbeatable."

Philadelphia's final statistics for the season were enough to scare any opponent—the 76ers were an awe-inspiring scoring machine. Wilt Chamberlain finished third in the league in scoring (behind Rick Barry and Oscar Robertson) with 1,956 points for a 24.1-point average, far below his 33.5-point average of the previous season and by far his lowest in eight years of professional basketball—but the reasons were obvious. Playing a team game, Wilt also finished third among the league's assist-makers, with an average of 7.8 per game. He was the champion rebounder, grabbing 1,957, averaging 24.2 rebounds per game. His nearest rival, Bill Russell, snared 1,700 for a 21.0 average. And Big Wilt also led all the rest in the field goal percentage competition, as he scored at a percentage of .683. Not only did he set a new record for field goal percentage, Chamberlain also set a season's record for most assists by a center, 702—a definite indicator of a team player.

Joining Wilt in the select circle of scoring leaders were teammates Hal Greer (sixth place with

The "new" Wilt Chamberlain added defense to his many other talents. Here he blocks a shot by the Celtics' Tom Sanders.

CHAMPIONS
BOSTON CELTICS
BOSTON CELTICS
BOSTON CELTICS
CELTICS 16
PHILA 54
CELTICS 24

a 22.1-points-per-game average), Chet Walker (12th in the league with 19.3), and Billy Cunningham (15th place with 18.5).

Before the Boston-Philadelphia confrontation each team had to defeat lesser challengers in the first round of the playoffs. This they did with ease. Boston crunched a fine Knickerbocker team, three games to one. Philadelphia matched this effort by stopping the Cincinnati Royals in three out of four.

Boston had one of the great teams in basketball history and it was seeking its ninth straight championship. Center Bill Russell was the greatest defensive center ever to play the game. In addition, the Celtics had the great defensive play of veteran guard K. C. Jones, the reliable shooting and playmaking of Sam Jones and the tireless all-court efforts of forward-guard John Havlicek. It looked as if the 76ers would have their hands full.

The series went decisively to Philadelphia. Sam Jones and John Havlicek, Boston's best scorers, missed the basket again and again. K. C. Jones kept losing Hal Greer, who seemed to score at will. Giant rebounders Bill Russell and Satch Sanders seemed to grow smaller with each game in the shadow of Wilt Chamberlain. In one game Big Wilt swamped Boston by clearing the boards of 41 rebounds, a playoff record. After that contest, an exhausted Chamberlain told reporters, "I've never moved so much in my life. Not even the night I scored 100."

And so, Philadelphia ended the Celtic string of eight straight championships by winning four out of five games in the series, including a smashing 140–116 victory in the fifth game. The next night in St. Louis, the San Francisco Warriors won the Western Division title by defeating the Hawks 112–107.

The championship series between Philadelphia and San Francisco was expected to be an anti-climax to the Boston-Philadelphia battle. How could San Francisco, a team that could manage no better than a 44–37 regular-season record, stay on the same floor with the magnificent men of Alex Hannum? Some observers expected the 76ers to sweep the series in four games. The Warriors had Rick Barry, a master scorer who had taken the league's scoring title, and Nate Thurmond, one of the top professional centers in rebounding and scoring. But the rest of the team was not so well-known, including such names as Paul Neumann, Fred Hetzel, Jeff Mullins (before he became a scoring leader), Tom Meschery, Jim King and so on.

Still, Alex Hannum refused to take the championship series lightly. Whether he was *seriously* concerned, no one but Hannum knew, but he expressed respect for the Warriors by stating, "If any team in the NBA has a chance to build a dynasty, it's San Francisco. We're stronger than the Warriors for the time being because Wilt Chamberlain and Hal Greer are still in their early years. Nevertheless, San Francisco has the best young talent in the league. They have the strong rebounder in Nate Thurmond and the strong scorer in Rick Barry, and they are patterned after the Celtics. The Warriors have a much better chance of dominating this league for the next 10 years than the 76ers do."

Those who doubted San Francisco's strength had to amend their thinking after the opening game. Although the 76ers won, 141–135, before a hometown crowd, they had to do it in overtime. Philadelphia might well have lost the game in the closing seconds of the fourth period if it had not been for Chamberlain.

All season long the Warriors had scored big on what they called their "bread-and-butter" play. It went this way: Rick Barry would drive to the key, leap into the air, then pass off to Thurmond as he moved toward the basket. This strategy often caught opposing guards and centers switching from one Warrior to another, and Thurmond collected two-pointers untouched. It was this play that Barry and Thurmond tried in the crucial closing seconds of the first championship playoff game—but Chamberlain refused to be suckered out of position. Instead, he blocked any possible pass to Thurmond while Barry was stuck with the ball in midair. Five minutes later the 76ers had their 6-point victory.

Two nights later, again at The Spectrum, Philadelphia didn't wait for the end to put on a show of last-ditch heroics. They bombed the Warriors for their second straight win, 126–95. As he had been all season long, Chamberlain was tremendous. He rebounded at both ends of the court. He passed off to his corner men or driving guards. He blocked shots and discouraged the Warriors from shooting because they were afraid he might block the ball. And whenever Philly needed a two-pointer, Wilt was the man they looked for: the ball would go to him in the lane, he'd whirl and stuff it home.

But it was not all Chamberlain. Wally Jones showed strongly as a playmaker, defensive stalwart and dependable scorer. Hal Greer proved to be better than ever, prompting one sportswriter to rave, "He was brilliant at times and never less than steady." Luke Jackson also made his weight felt, storming the backboards and pumping in points as part of the well-balanced 76er attack.

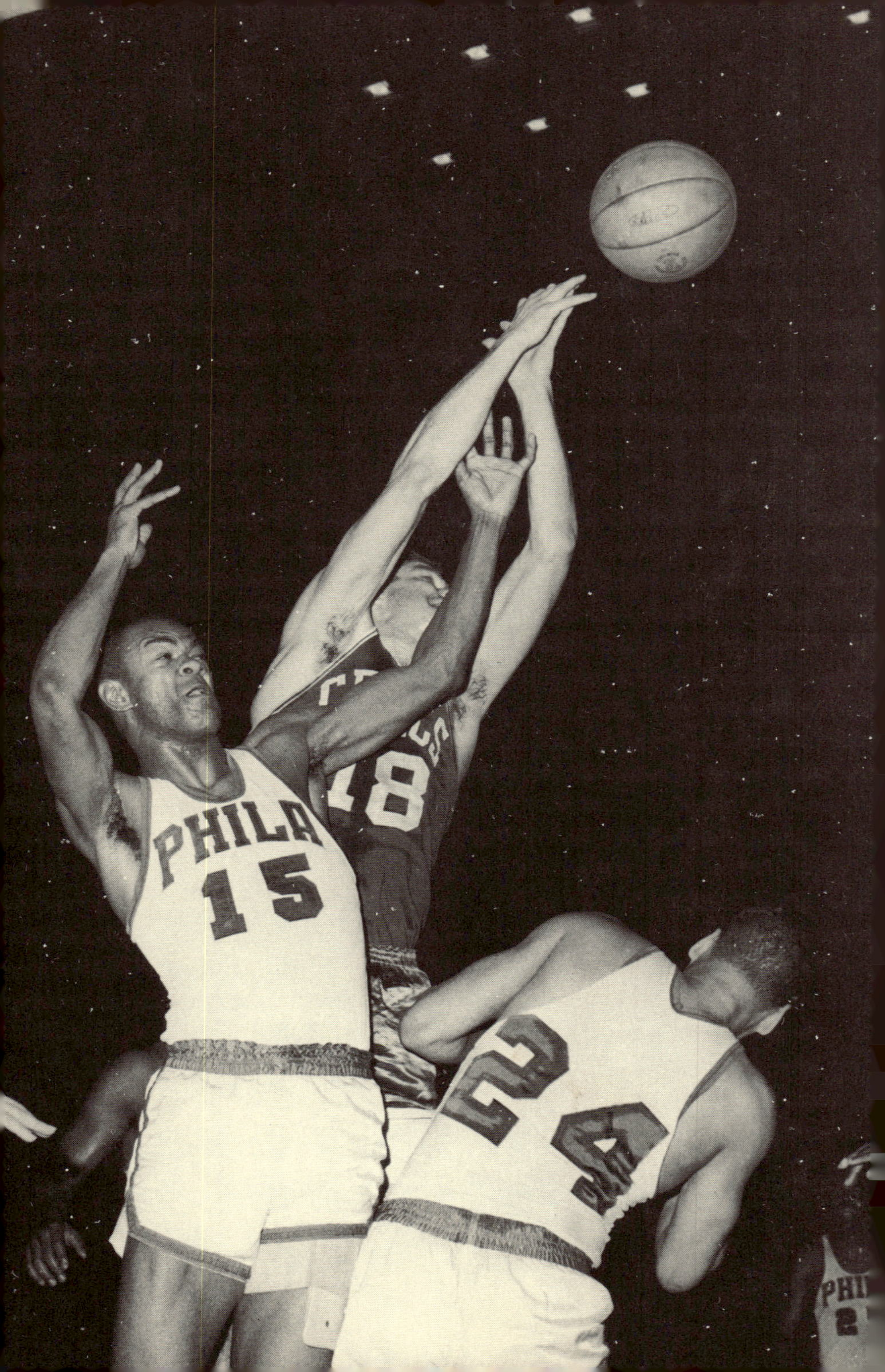
PHILA
15
18
24

PHILADELPHIA 76ERS, 1966–67

Chet Walker pounded away at the Warriors game after game, running, rebounding, shooting, setting picks and sticking to his man on defense like adhesive tape. Cunningham came off the bench with brilliant bursts of scoring whenever the 76ers needed a pickup in point production.

The next game was scheduled two days later, in San Francisco, and the Warriors put the time to good use. They spent part of each practice session shooting over tennis racquets held high in front of the basket. Rick Barry explained that they were trying to get a higher arch on their shots. "Wilt has been batting away too many. We have to get a higher arch," he said.

Whether the racquet technique was responsible, or the fact that they were two games behind and playing at home, the Warriors came fighting back to take the third game 130–124. Rick Barry made best use of his shooting skills as he ripped the nets for 55 points.

The next game, again at San Francisco, ended with the 76ers on top 122–108. Now they were one victory away from the championship. Barry had once more kept the underdogs in the fight, hitting for 41 of San Francisco's points. Chamberlain,

Hal Greer (15) was a mainstay of the 76ers' championship drive. Here he fights with Bailey Howell of the Celtics for the ball.

who was used to being the high scorer himself, had taken only six shots all night, none of them in the second half. Grinning at his new role as a rebounder and playmaker, Wilt observed wryly, "Sometimes it's actually easier to play against a team that has one man do most of the shooting." In the past such remarks had always been leveled at Wilt. Now he was on the other side.

The fifth game was played back in Philadelphia, where the Warriors staved off final defeat by beating the 76ers 117–109. Now they were behind in the series 3–2. If they could win one more game in Philadelphia, they could play the deciding game at home after winning two in a row.

Barry led the way for San Francisco, with 44 points, which won him the distinction of setting a new scoring mark: 251 points in the Warriors' 15 games. But Chamberlain was not to be denied. He rammed home 24 points, collected 23 rebounds, made four assists and intimidated Warrior shooters. Wilt contributed a big share to bring the 1967 NBA crown home to Philadelphia. The final score was 125–122, and again the 76ers gave a perfect example of the balanced team in action. Surprising San Francisco was leading 102–97 when the

Chamberlain shoots over the outstretched hand of Bill Russell in the final playoff series.

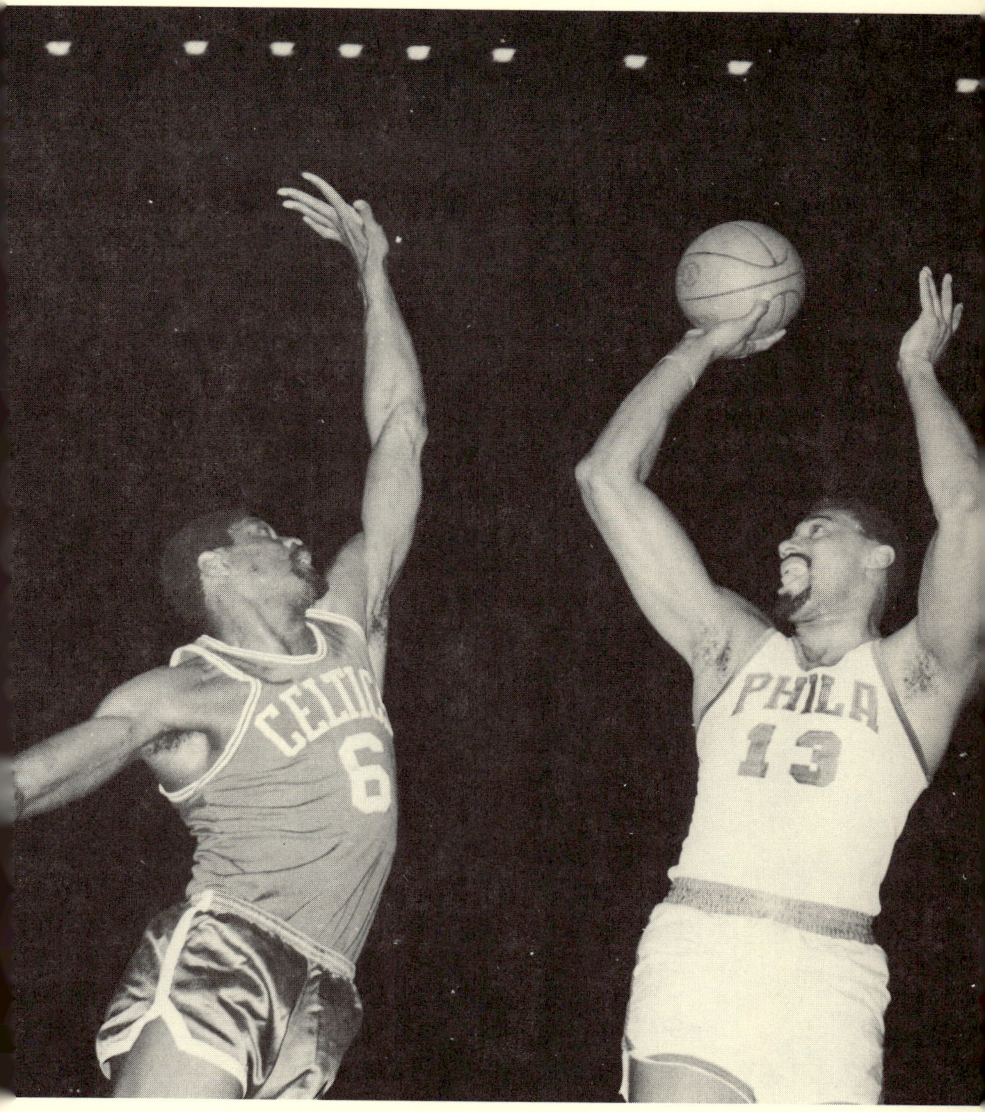

CELTIC
6
PHILA
13

fourth quarter opened, but at this point Philadelphia clamped down, checking the hot-handed Rick Barry and taking charge in the rebounding department. Feeding, scoring, rebounding and playing aggressive defense, Wilt led the 76ers to a 28–20 squelching of San Francisco in the last period, and that made all the difference. Wilt had finally proved he could be a winner!

PHILADELPHIA 76ERS, 1966–67

Philadelphia 76ers, 1966-67

Statistics
Regular season:
Team record: Won 68, lost 13. Finished first in Eastern Division.
Individual leaders:

	Games	Points	Points per Game	Rebounds	Assists
Chamberlain	81	1,956	24.1	1,957	630
Greer	80	1,765	22.1	422	303
Walker	81	1,567	19.3	660	188
Cunningham	81	1,495	18.5	589	205

Playoff record:
First round, vs. Cincinnati (best 3 out of 5)

Philadelphia	116	CINCINNATI	120
PHILADELPHIA	123	Cincinnati	102
PHILADELPHIA	121	Cincinnati	106
PHILADELPHIA	112	Cincinnati	94

Second round, vs. Boston (best 4 out of 7)

PHILADELPHIA	127	Boston	113
PHILADELPHIA	107	Boston	102
PHILADELPHIA	115	Boston	104
Philadelphia	117	BOSTON	121
PHILADELPHIA	140	Boston	116

GREAT TEAMS OF PRO BASKETBALL

Championship round, vs. San Francisco (best 4 out of 7)

PHILADELPHIA	141*	San Francisco	135
PHILADELPHIA	126	San Francisco	95
Philadelphia	124	SAN FRANCISCO	130
PHILADELPHIA	122	San Francisco	108
Philadelphia	109	SAN FRANCISCO	117
PHILADELPHIA	125	San Francisco	122

* Overtime game.

Boston Celtics 1968-69

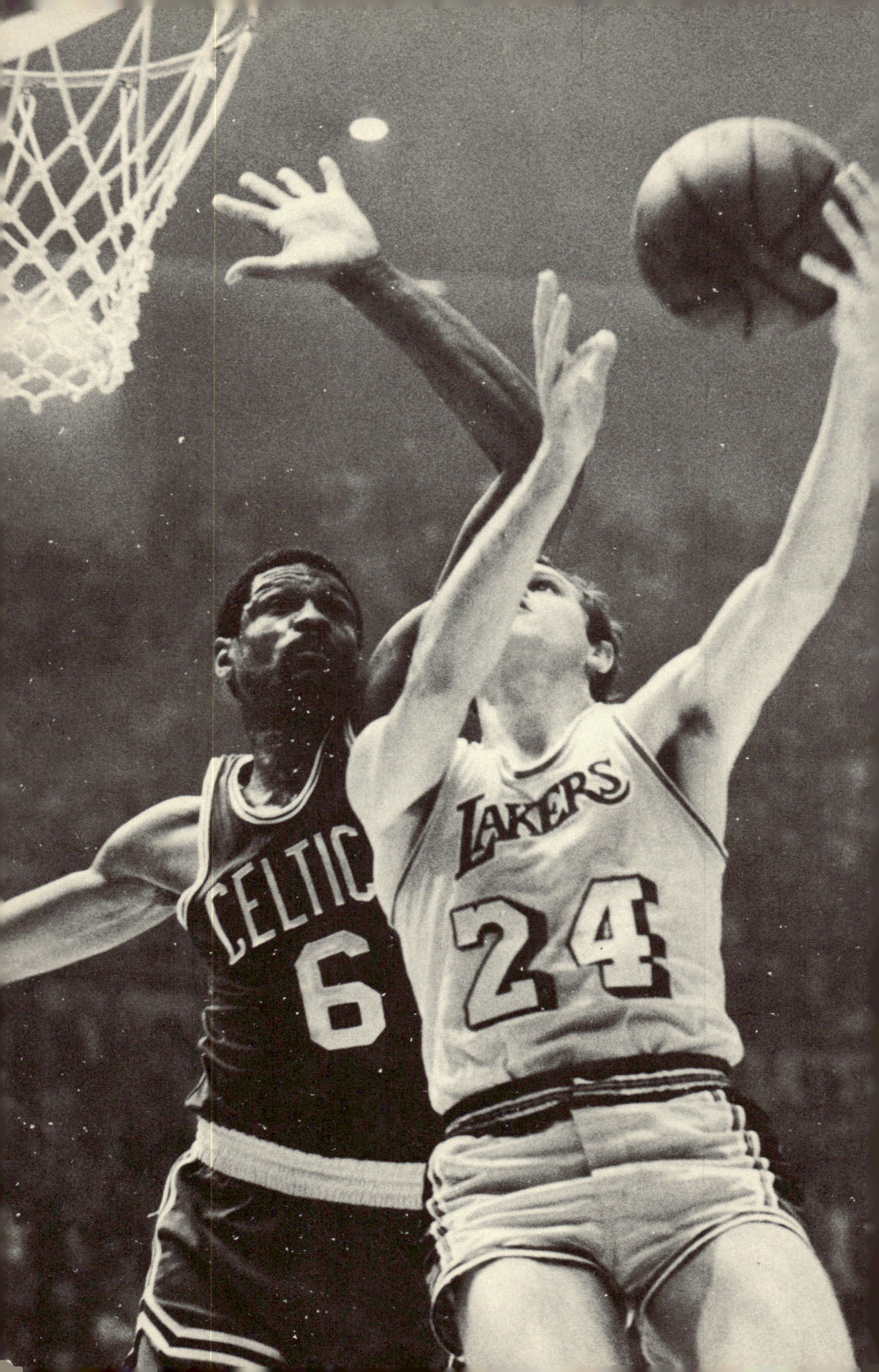
CELTIC
6
LAKERS
24

Bill Russell, the center of the Boston Celtics, prepares to slap away a shot by the Lakers' Keith Erickson.

At the beginning of the 1968–69 professional basketball season, the Boston Celtics were the possessors of an enviable record. They had won ten NBA championships in the last twelve years and had become a sports dynasty, a succession of teams that had dominated the sport almost completely. Bill Russell, who had recently become player-coach of the Celtics, had been a pivotal part of their success since joining the Celtics in 1956. With Russell at center, the Celtics had failed only twice to win the NBA title, once in 1957–58 when they lost to St. Louis, and once in 1966–67 when the Philadelphia 76ers took the crown.

But in the fall of 1968, the Celtics were not the team they had been in previous years. Their key players were aging rapidly (indeed, Russell and Sam Jones would retire at the end of the season). Basketball writers and fans doubted the team could continue its long winning tradition. "The Celtic dynasty is dead. Bring on the new king," wrote one sports columnist.

The NBA was certainly filled with potential champions. Sportswriter Berry Stainback picked the New York Knicks to win in Boston's Eastern Division. One strong contender, Philadelphia, had traded away Wilt Chamberlain, weakening their chances. As for Boston, Stainback was convinced that they had "too much age on the court and too little strength on the bench."

The Knicks were strong, boasting a fine young squad that beat its opponents with speed and defense. Still, even Philadelphia without Chamberlain looked stronger than Boston. And even if the Celts could take first place in the East, they would probably face the fabulous Los Angeles Lakers in the championship. The Lakers had not one or two, but three superstars—Wilt Chamberlain, Elgin Baylor and Jerry West.

A review of the Celtic line-up appeared to confirm dire predictions about their future. Russell was due to turn 35 in midseason and he had the heavy responsibility of coaching the team as well as playing for it. High-scoring guard Sam Jones was 36, and forwards Bailey Howell and Tom "Satch" Sanders were both past 30. Reserve center Wayne Embry, who might have relieved

Russell, had been lost to an expansion team, so Howell and Sanders were being counted on to take over more of the rebounding burden. John Havlicek, who had been the league's best "sixth man"—a versatile substitute who could replace either guards or forwards—was expected to be in the starting five at guard. This took the sting out of Boston's previous ability to send him in, fresh and strong, for a quick boost to their feared running attack. Veteran Larry Siegfried would be there again to provide reliable defense and about 14 points a game. The rest of the team was either near retirement or young and inexperienced.

Early in the season the Celtics won a few and lost a few. Fortunately for their chances, the other teams in the league had been weakened by the expansion draft in which each team had to give up players to two new NBA clubs. The new teams themselves, the Milwaukee Bucks and the Phoenix Suns, gave many easy victories to the stronger teams in the league.

The Celts won four and lost two in October. They won 11 and lost four in November. December brought a tougher stretch of games and the Celts could do no better than win seven and lose six. January turned out to be their last strong month as they posted 12 wins against six losses. Age was beginning to show, especially when Bos-

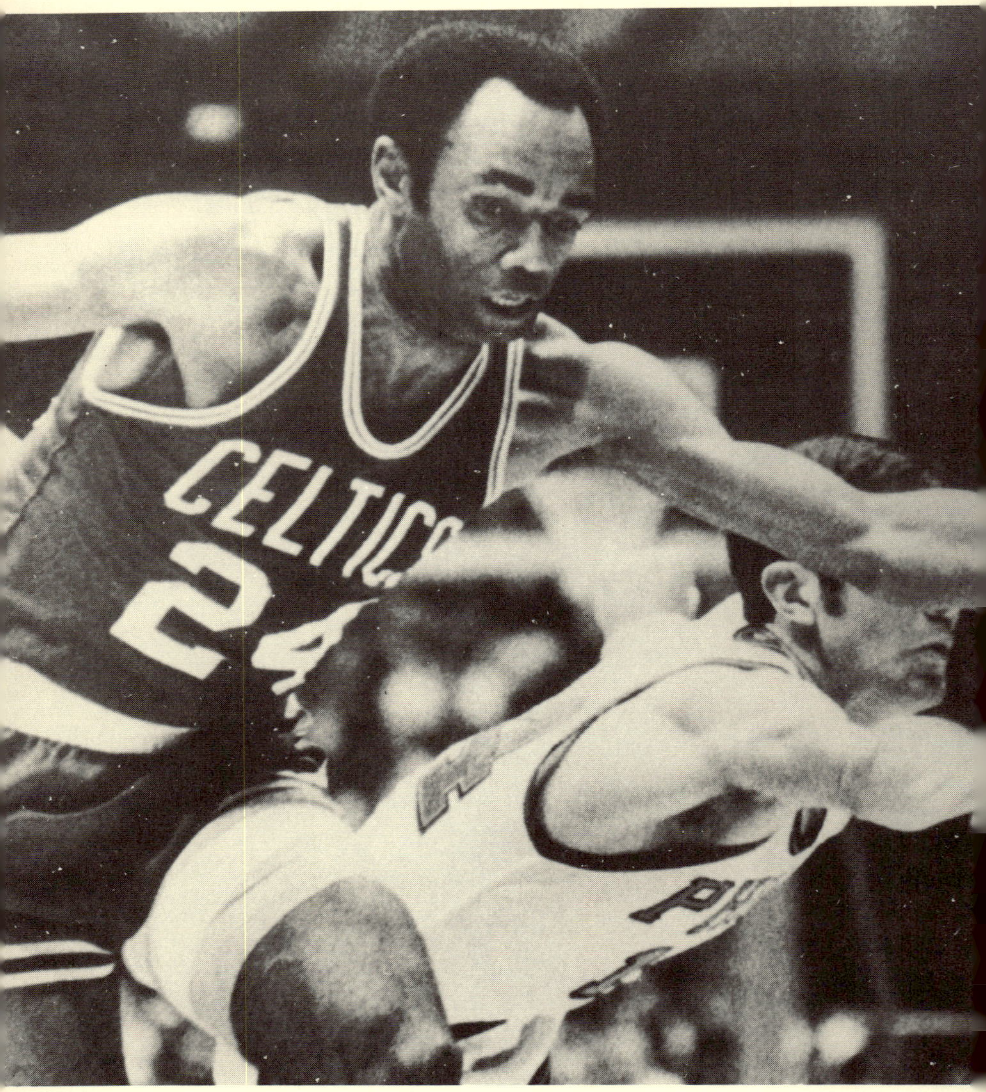
CELTICS
24

Sam Jones, playing his last year for the Celtics, fights the 76ers' Matt Guokas for the ball.

ton fought to keep pace with speed-oriented clubs such as the Knicks, Bullets and 76ers. Sam Jones spent more time on the bench, letting the inexhaustible John Havlicek and experienced Larry Siegfried replace him at guard. Russell kept himself out more often, too, while burly Jim Barnes or Satch Sanders covered center.

Still, every now and then there was a hopeful sign. Jones' point production had dropped from 21 points per game in past years to about 16, but he could be counted on to come in during the closing minutes of a tight game and start pouring in clutch baskets. And Russell could still menace an entire team with his presence as the supreme shot-blocker. As Jerry West said after a Los Angeles-Boston game, "Russell doesn't even have to be there. You always have the sense of him being there. I don't think anybody dominates a game so much as he does, or controls it so much."

Further testimony came from Bill Cunningham, the high-scoring forward of the Philadelphia 76ers. "I remember one game Russell played against us that year," he said. "The Celtics had lost five or six in a row when he was out with an injury. Barnes was playing center and got into foul trouble real quick. We were 12 in front. It looked like a breeze.

"Finally, Bill took himself off the bench and put

himself into the game. He hobbled onto the court, but as soon as he came in, you could see the Celtics' heads get higher. That old man seemed to pump confidence into them as though they were saying to themselves, 'Now we can come back and win.'

"Right after that, the first play, there's a two-shot foul against us. Russell is lined up next to me on the foul line. I say to him, 'How's your leg?' He looks so sad. You know, that bedraggled, drawn look on his face. This time he looks like a caricature of himself. 'Boy,' he says, 'I have this pain in my leg, it shoots all the way down to my toes.'

"They make the first foul shot, but the second bounds off the back of the rim. I go up. He goes up way over me and dunks in the basket. What can I tell you? He hurts so much he's killing me. I tell him, 'I bleed for you,' and I'm bleeding for us. The last play of regulation time he leads a fast break. He gets thrown a high pass, so high that when he goes up his shoulders are over the basket, and he stuffs it in to tie the game. Then they go on to beat us in overtime."

And Cunningham's teammate, Hal Greer, added, "Even when I have a pick to shoot from behind, I still have to jump back and shoot higher to get the ball over Russell. He always seems to be around."

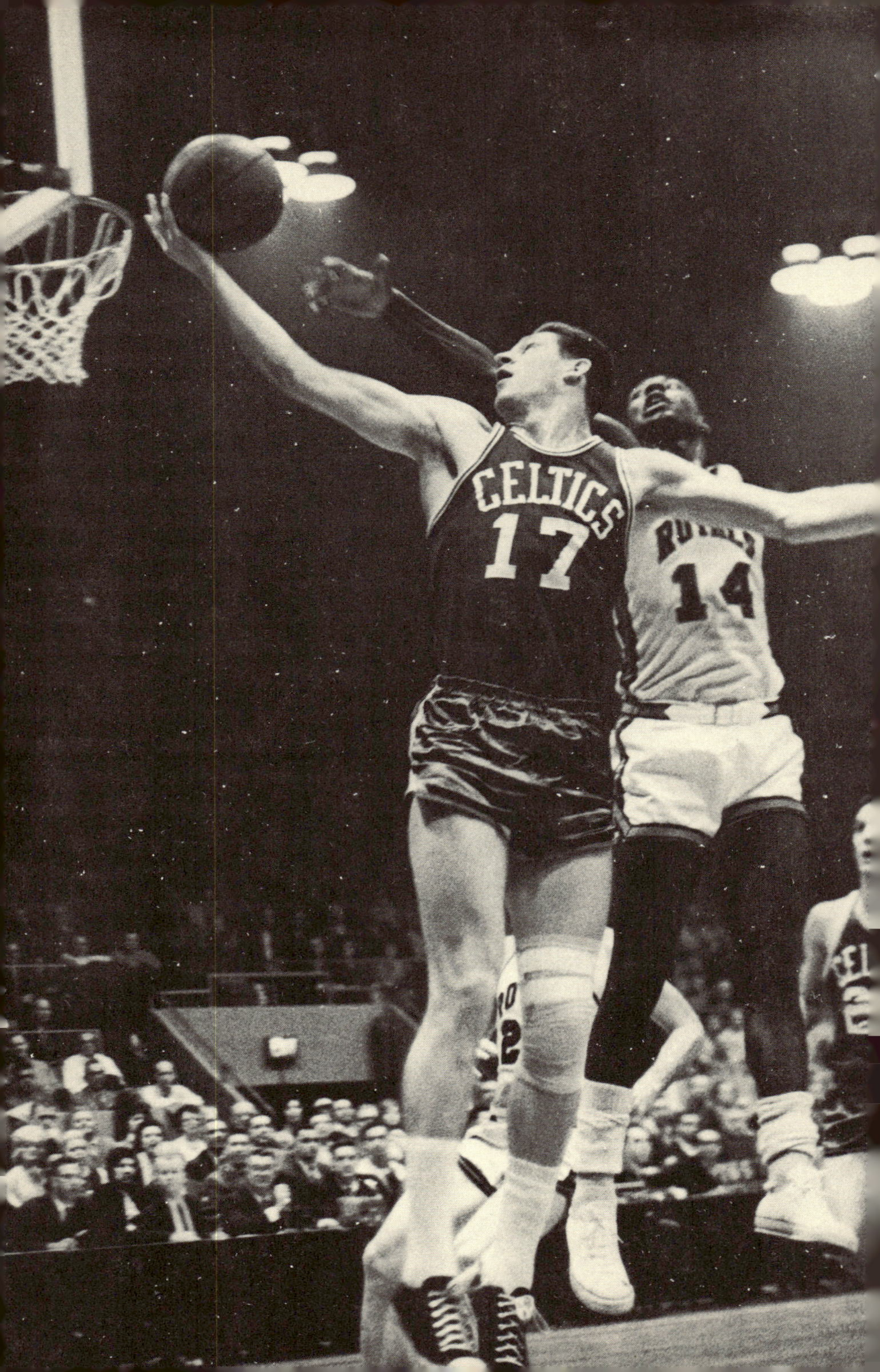
CELTICS
17
ROYALS
14

BOSTON CELTICS, 1968–69

Another factor that kept the Celtics in contention was pride. No man on the team had more of it than John Havlicek. He once said, "Pride is the thing that can push you." So deeply did he feel this pride in his team and himself that even Bill Russell felt its force. In one game Boston's fast pace was being matched by the opposing team. Russell began falling behind.

As Havlicek recalled it, "Russell would clear a defensive rebound and then loaf up the court so that we'd have to play four-on-five until he got there. 'Russell, run!' I'd yell from the bench whenever he didn't hustle up on offense. 'You're no good to us if you don't come up the floor!'"

And Russell would hustle each time. "I need that kind of push," he said. "I hope John never stops reminding me." Russell and the rest of the team followed Havlicek's lead—they had a compelling desire to win.

The Celtics still seemed to have little chance at the league title, but they were doing better than many had predicted. Russell was one factor. Pride was another. And another was defense.

Defense had always been emphasized by Boston's former coach, Red Auerbach. (He had be-

Pushed by his pride in himself and the team, John Havlicek scores on a lay-up against Oscar Robertson.

come the Celtics' general manager and he turned the coaching job over to Bill Russell.) The way the Celtics had played under Auerbach and continued to play under Russell, an opponent with the ball had to get past three men on his way to the basket. If he managed to overcome this defensive picket line, he still faced another obstacle—a sinewy, 6'9" wall of defense with large hands, split-second timing and impeccable intuition, named Bill Russell. The Celtic formula of closing up the middle approach to the basket showed a high percentage of success. They put the heaviest pressure on their opponents' best players and forced them to pass to a weaker or less-experienced offensive player. No matter who was driving for the basket, Boston would put a three-pronged squeeze on him. It was a style of defense that cooled many a hot team and gave Boston victories over clubs that seemed superior on paper.

The Auerbach style, followed religiously by Russell, was conceded by enemy coaches to be worth at least 10 points a game to the Celtics. Russell drilled the concept of defense into his team in preseason training and continued the drills in practice sessions between games. During the games the Celtic philosophy was defense. As Auerbach had expressed it: "I'll let a man rest on offense, but not on defense. If I see him loafing, out he comes. With Russell on this club, we're a step ahead of the rest of the league on defense, and I mean to keep us there."

A good example of the Boston style occurred in a game against the Baltimore Bullets. The Bullets, who finished first in the Eastern Division during the regular season, also relied on a running game. They had two sharpshooting guards, Earl Monroe and Kevin Loughery, and a strong center, Wes Unseld. But in this particular game they were the second best team on the floor because they couldn't contain Russell nor break the Celtic defense.

A typical moment in the game illustrates how the Celtics could overpower a team. The Bullets lead by one. Baltimore's Leroy Ellis takes the ball and passes to Monroe. Monroe moves across midcourt, veers to his left and starts his drive. Havlicek intercepts him and slaps at the ball. Monroe loses it and Boston recovers. Havlicek dribbles straight ahead, then passes to Sam Jones who moves from the top of the key to the corner, stops and whips the ball out to Russell in the open. Russell drives, hooks and scores.

Monroe brings the ball up for Baltimore. He waves Loughery and Marin into position for a set play. Em Bryant and Havlicek are pressing him, but Earl snaps the ball to Kevin Loughery and he dribbles once, twice, then goes up for the shot—but Russell leaps high and blocks it. Bryant recovers the ball for Boston, passes it to Havlicek and the Celtics have a three-on-two fast break. Havlicek passes cross-court to Jones, who drives, stops, shoots a ten-foot jumper and misses. Russell goes up for the rebound and rams the ball into the hoop. The Celtics go ahead by three and Baltimore brings the ball up slowly, their attack blunted by Boston's tight defense.

Boston won that game, but the demands of the exhausting schedule on the older players were showing more and more. Weariness was wearing down the team and their February record reflected it: the Celtics could win only seven games while losing nine. March was not much better, as the club managed to win half of the remaining 14 games before the playoffs were scheduled to begin.

The final standings for the regular 1968–69 season showed Baltimore in first place in the Eastern Division, followed by Philadelphia, New York and Boston. The Celtics barely qualified for a playoff spot with a 48–34 won-loss record.

It looked like the end of the line for the Celts

An exhausted Bill Russell, responsible for coaching the team and playing on it, takes a rest.

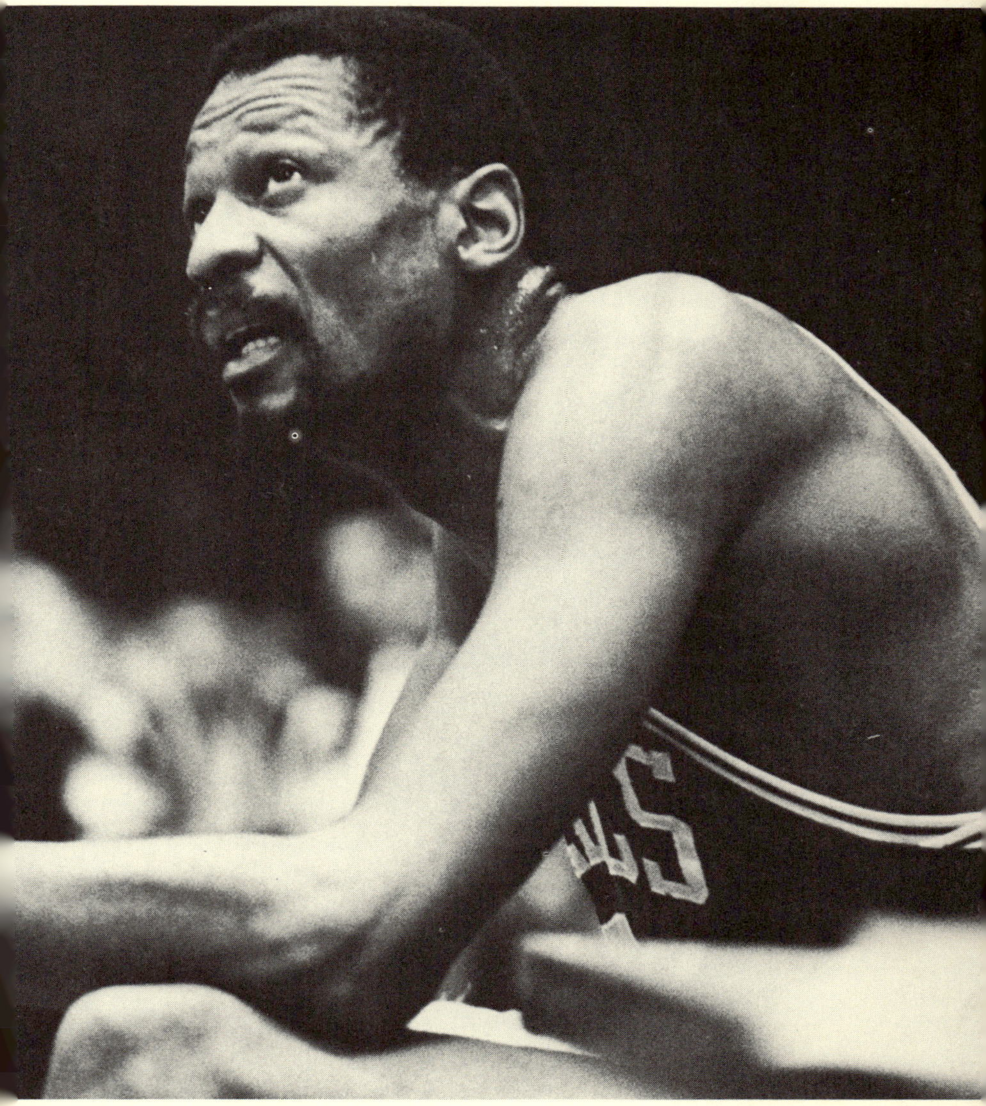

when they took the floor against the Philadelphia 76ers in the first round of the playoffs. Philadelphia had made a strong showing in the regular season. But the 76ers didn't have Wilt Chamberlain, who had been traded to Los Angeles, and Boston did have Bill Russell. And that, to the dismay of the 76ers, made all the difference.

In the first game, Boston clobbered the 76ers 114–100. Russell, showing strength, stamina and that old-time pride, played as if he were ten years younger. He was the undisputed master of the rebounds and a monumental defensive force. Bailey Howell was right in there, too, working the boards with his coach. And even more effective was the rebounding of John Havlicek, regarded more as a playmaker and scorer than a rebounder.

In the regular season Havlicek had made only 570 rebounds while scoring at a substantial 21.6-points-per-game average. In fact he had led the Celtics in scoring. Behind him had come Bailey Howell, who had notched an average of 19.7 points per game over the season, followed by Sam Jones with 16.3 and Larry Siegfried with 14.2.

This relatively low scoring accurately described the Celtics—a team that was far more of a threat on defense than offense. Yet they had topped Philadelphia by 14 points in the first playoff game. And that was just the beginning. They met the

76ers at Boston Garden two days later and treated more than 15,000 home fans to a 134–103 win. Again it was Russell, Havlicek, Jones and Howell —and defense.

Two days later the Celtics made it three in a row, downing the 76ers in Philadelphia, 125–118. The Celtics' delight was expressed by one Boston fan who was traveling with the team: "For a bunch of ancient has-beens we're looking pretty good, aren't we?"

Philadelphia rallied to squeak out a 119–116 victory over the Celtics in the fourth game. But Boston wrapped up the series in the fifth game, beating the 76ers 93–90, much to the disappointment of the 76er fans at The Spectrum.

Meanwhile, the tenacious New York Knicks had met the first-place Baltimore Bullets. In an amazing upset, the Knicks steam-rollered the Bullets in four straight by scores of 113–101, 107–91, 119–116 and 115–108. Thus the Eastern Division championship would go either to the Celtics or to the Knicks, a team that played the Celtic style of defensive game but with a roster of much younger players. The starting line-up of Willis Reed, Walt Frazier, Dick Barnett, Dave DeBusschere and Bill Bradley meant speed, defense honed to perfection, and stamina. The five Knick starters also had better scoring credentials than any five Celtics. Although the Knick bench was weak New York was favored to take the series.

The Celts upset the odds by trouncing the Knicks 108–100 in the first game, on the Knicks' home court. In their second meeting, at Boston, the Celtics went two-up on the strength of a 112–97 victory. Basketball writer Frank Deford examined the collapse of the Knicks in this second game. "The Knicks went six minutes and 20 seconds without a basket and ended up with only 14 points in the first quarter," he pointed out. "Then they went cold. They were shut out for the first 4:50 of the second period and had made but three of 33 attempted baskets to that point. With only 2:16 left in the half, Boston still had more than twice as many points as New York, 49 to 24."

Boston's wins were even more impressive because they had lost six of seven games to the Knicks during the regular season. Several of the Knicks voiced the same thought after the second loss. "The next game's back on our floor," they said. "Now we're due for a run of good luck—you can't keep shooting and not start to connect. That's what the law of averages is all about." The Knick shots did fall in with more regularity in the third contest and New York made the series 2–1 with a 101–91 win at Madison Square Garden.

The fourth game in the best-of-seven series was

BOSTON CELTICS, 1968–69

again at Boston, and it was a tense, hard-fought battle. Both teams concentrated on defense, working for the good shot, and trying to outfox the opposition. Playing top-grade basketball, Boston finally gained the victory, 97–96. The two teams prepared for game number five, at New York, with the Knicks down 3–1.

To men who know basketball best, the almost unbelievable was happening. The Celtics, those tired and ancient fourth-place finishers, were on the edge of winning the second round of the playoffs and qualifying for the championship series. Although they had their weakest team in years, they were still playing championship basketball. The Knicks took the fifth game 112–104 at home. But they still trailed three games to two, and to have a chance, they would have to even up the series by winning the sixth game in Boston.

The sixth game was bitter, bruising basketball all the way. Neither team gained a comfortable lead until the Celtics opened up a healthy margin in the fourth quarter. Then the Knicks came back and soon were challenging for the lead. The Boston fans jumped to their feet as the Knicks cut the

Cool and controlled, John Havlicek drives through the Philadelphia defense. ➤

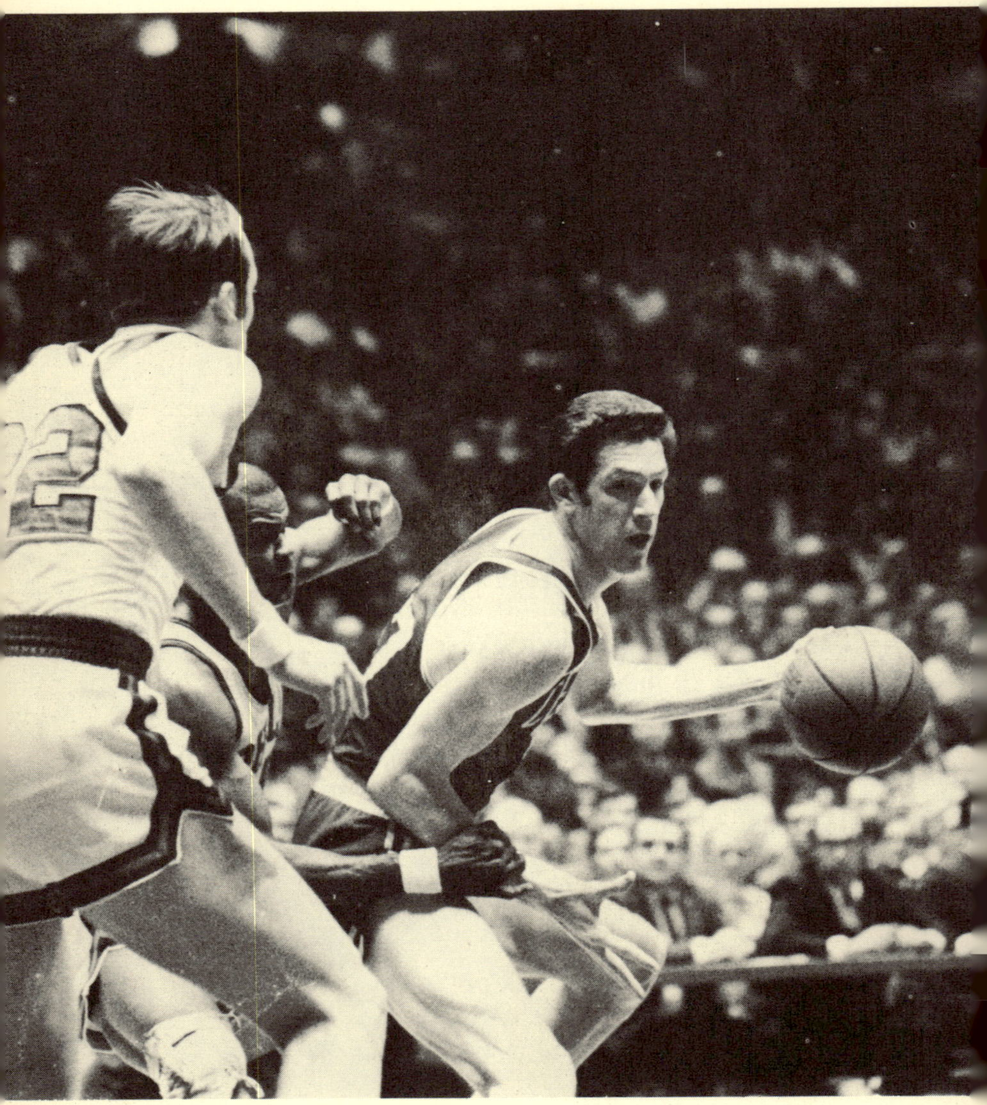

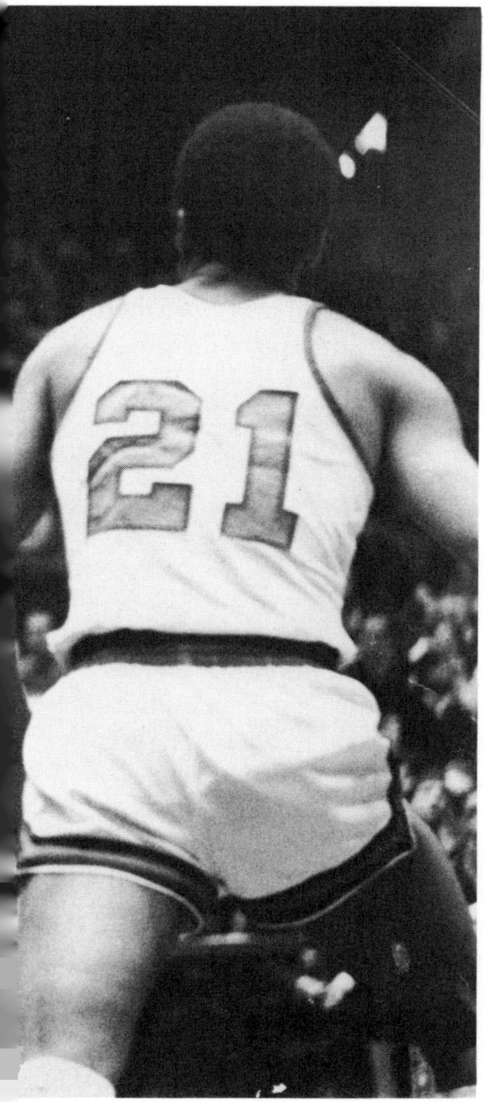
21

Boston lead to one basket. Then the Celtics scored again to take a four-point advantage.

Throughout the game Russell seemed to time his shots to do the most psychological damage to the Knicks. But Russell was not the hero of the closing minutes of the game. The basket that pushed the score to 103–99, Celtics, was described by Russell as a "crazy, wild, unbelievable shot." The one that made it 105–101 and sewed up the game was a masterpiece of suspense. The man who made both of them was the cool, self-assured veteran, John Havlicek.

With the score 103–101, Boston was moving the ball, keeping it away from the desperate Knicks, and eating up the last seconds. Havlicek got the ball with fewer than 10 seconds left on the 24-second clock. If the Knicks got the ball before Boston scored, New York could tie the game. Havlicek held the ball over his head, then he faked left, faked right, faked again and started to dribble. Bill Bradley was hounding him and the Boston faithful were shouting, "Shoot!" Havlicek glanced up at the clock. It showed just five seconds. Havlicek used up three more seconds driving to the baseline, then let go an off-balance, almost impossible one-hander.

The ball swished through the net and the Knicks' last hope for making the championship series died. "Baby, I can't believe it!" gasped Larry Siegfried.

"In my first year or two in the NBA," Havlicek said after the game, "I would have taken the long shot from 15 feet out. But I've been in plenty of games like this in seven years, and I knew what I was doing."

Havlicek and his Celtic teammates had earned everybody's respect—and the right to meet the Los Angeles Lakers for the NBA championship. While Boston was defeating the 76ers and Knicks, the Lakers had conquered San Francisco four games to two, then beat Atlanta in five games.

Once again Chamberlain and Russell met in a playoff series. But this time Big Wilt had Jerry West and Elgin Baylor playing alongside him. Against these three basketball superstars, the Celtics were again heavy underdogs. Their fans almost gave up hope after the Lakers, playing on their home court, beat Boston twice, 120–118 and 118–112.

In both fiercely fought contests Chamberlain and Russell battered each other in the war for rebounds. And in both games Havlicek kept the Celtics in contention, netting 37 points in the first contest, 43 in the second. However, Jerry West overshadowed the Celts, hitting for 53 points in the first game and 41 in the second. "In that first

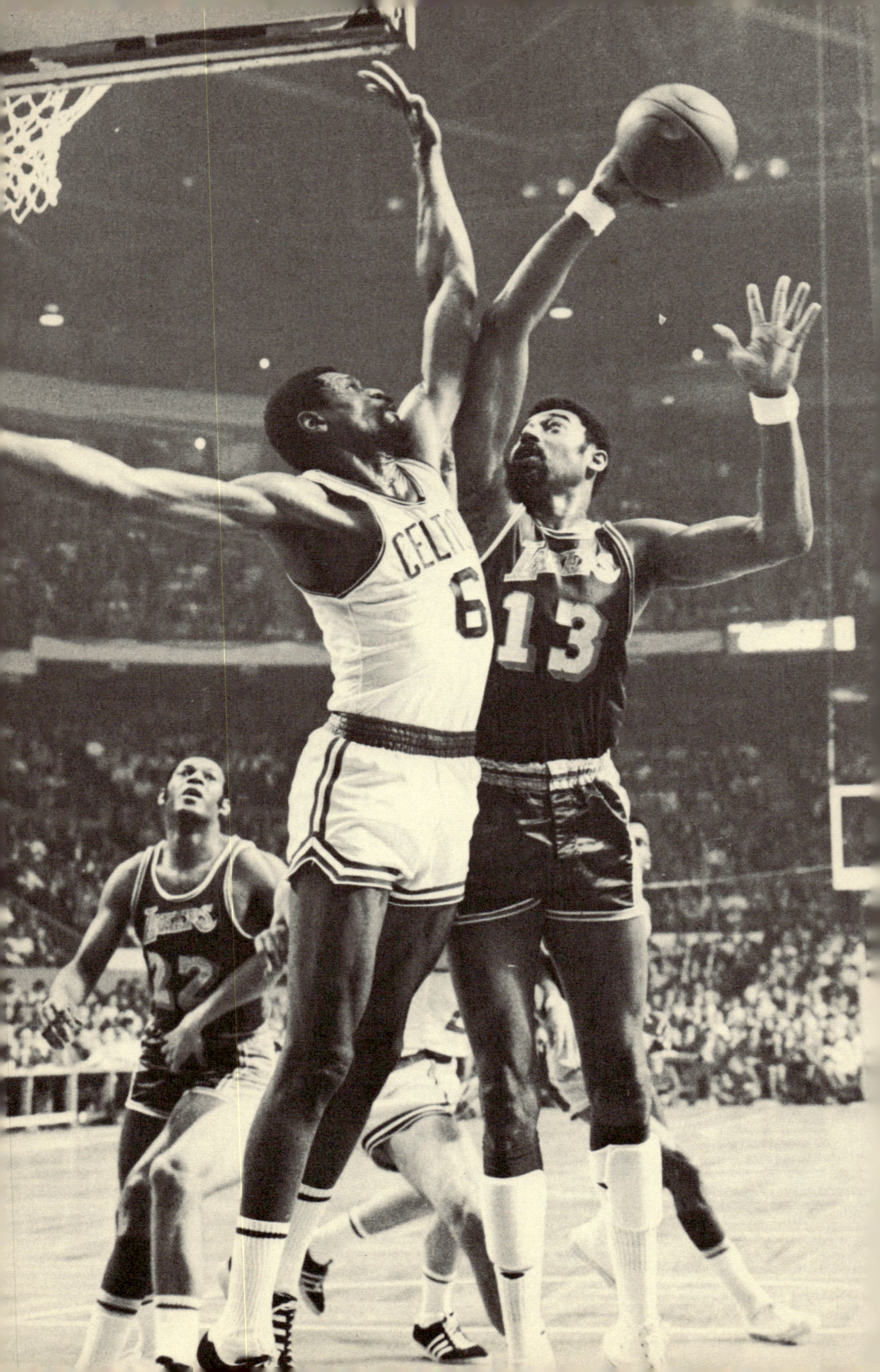
6
13

BOSTON CELTICS, 1968–69

game," Russell said afterward, "Jerry West gave the greatest clutch performance I have ever seen anyone ever give against the Celtics."

But the tide shifted when the two teams resumed the series in Boston. Again, Russell's board-work and Havlicek's shooting made the difference. In the third game of the series, John rang up 38 points in the Celtics' 111–105 win. In the fourth game he was top Celtic with 21 points as Boston won by the narrow margin of 89–88. Havlicek had to share miracle-man honors in this one with Sam Jones, who fired in the game-winning shot with only three seconds left in the game. It was one of the most awkward-looking shots ever taken in championship play—Jones had stumbled just before launching the shot—but it went through and that was all that mattered.

The teams were tied at two games apiece when action began again on May 1st at the Forum in Los Angeles. This time the Lakers applied the pressure and Russell, in particular, seemed to be running out of steam as the Lakers grabbed a crucial series lead with a 117–104 victory.

The Celtics had their backs against the wall. To

Two great centers meet again as Russell blocks a shot by Wilt Chamberlain.

win, they needed two games in a row. Playing at home, Boston took game six, 99–90. This left the seventh game, to be played in Los Angeles, to determine who would be the NBA's champion. By this time Boston had become the sentimental favorite, but Los Angeles had the advantage of playing at home.

Russell and Chamberlain met once more at center court and shook hands. The ball went up and the deciding 48 minutes of play had begun. The Celtics turned on the steam immediately, building a big lead that carried for a good part of the game. But Jerry West kept the Lakers alive with bucket after bucket and Chamberlain chipped in his share of field goals.

With three minutes to go in the fourth quarter, the Celtic lead had been whittled to a single point: they led 103–102. Still, the tired old Celtics managed to hang on. Russell, Havlicek and Sam Jones combined once again in the crucial moments, and the Celtics nipped the Lakers 108–106.

The Celtics had written a new chapter in the book of unforgettable comebacks. After a series of 18 grueling playoff games, they had come out on

Playing the last game of his career, Sam Jones goes up for two points in the deciding game of the championship series. Boston beat Philadelphia 108–106.

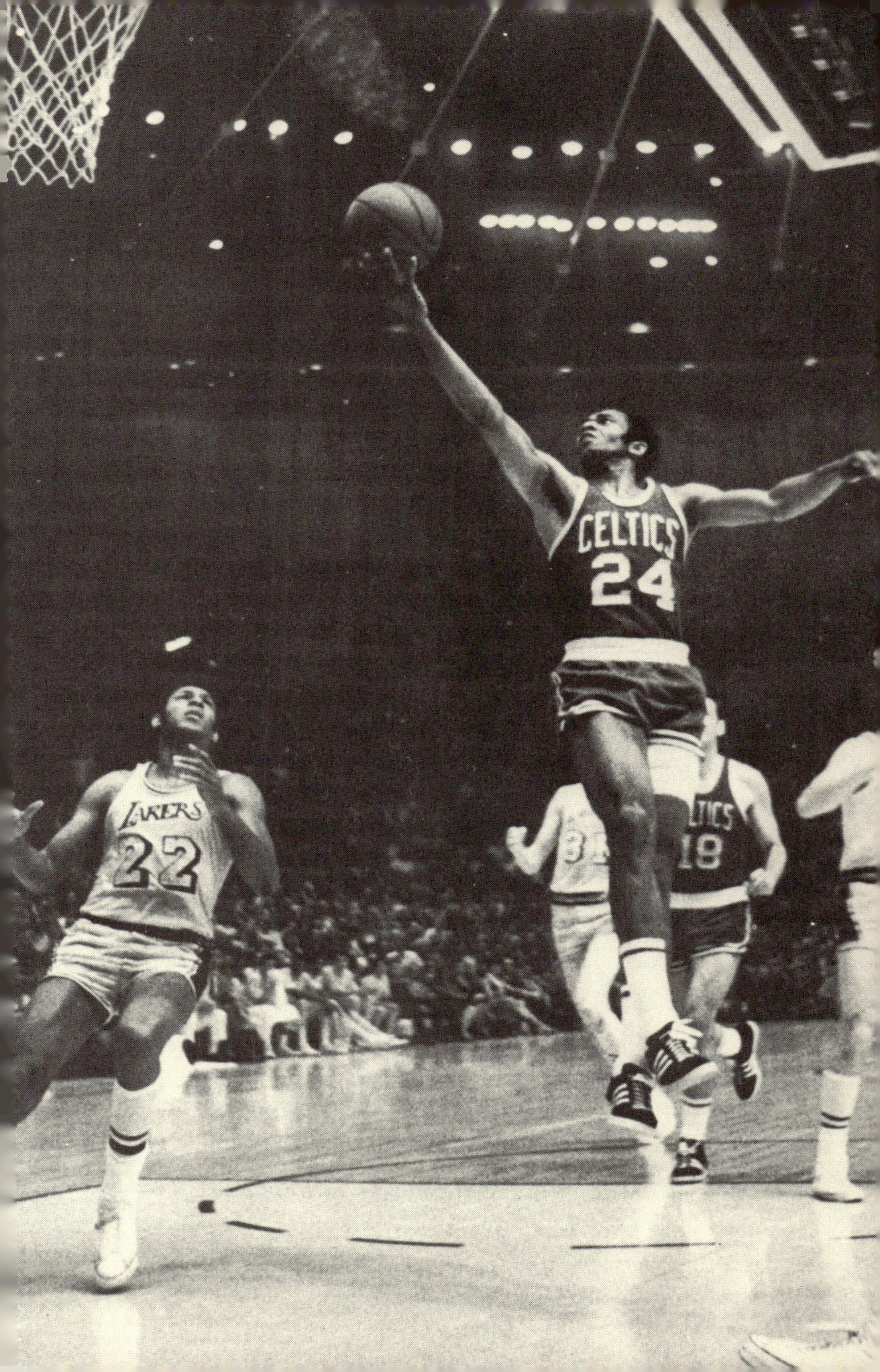
CELTICS
24
LAKERS
22
CELTICS
18

top thanks to one last effort from Bill Russell and Sam Jones, and to the continuing brilliance of Boston's Running Machine, John Havlicek. It took more than skill and determination to forge a victory out of the fierce combat of the 1969 playoffs. It took a huge measure of that Celtic quality for which Russell, Jones and Havlicek will be remembered: pride.

Boston Celtics, 1968-69

Statistics
Regular season:
Team record: Won 48, lost 34. Finished fourth in Eastern Division.
Individual leaders:

	Games	Points	Points per Game	Rebounds	Assists
Havlicek	82	1,771	21.6	570	141
Howell	78	1,537	19.7	685	137
Jones	70	1,140	16.3	265	182
Russell	77	762	9.9	1,484	374

Playoff record:
First round, vs. Philadelphia (best 4 out of 7)
BOSTON	114	Philadelphia	100
BOSTON	134	Philadelphia	103
BOSTON	125	Philadelphia	118
Boston	116	PHILADELPHIA	119
BOSTON	93	Philadelphia	90

Second round, vs. New York (best 4 out of 7)
BOSTON	108	New York	100
BOSTON	112	New York	97
Boston	91	NEW YORK	101
BOSTON	97	New York	96
Boston	104	NEW YORK	112
BOSTON	106	New York	105

Championship round, vs. Los Angeles (best 4 out of 7)

Boston	118	LOS ANGELES	120
Boston	112	LOS ANGELES	118
BOSTON	111	Los Angeles	105
BOSTON	89	Los Angeles	88
Boston	104	LOS ANGELES	117
BOSTON	99	Los Angeles	90
BOSTON	108	Los Angeles	106

New York Knicks 1969-70

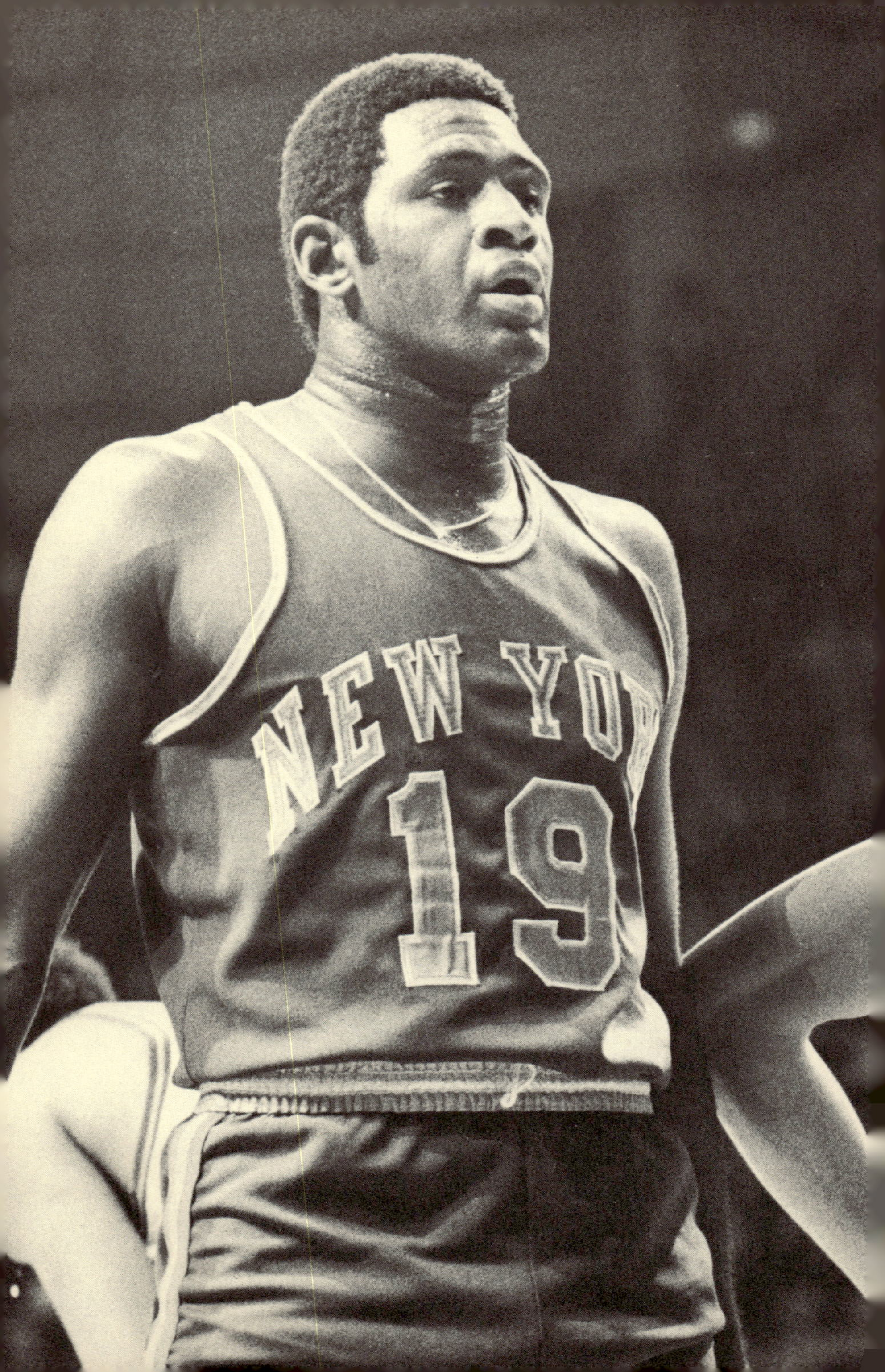
NEW YORK
19

Knick center Willis Reed, the man who was nearly indispensable.

Most NBA champions have been led by one or more of those very special players—the superstars. The great Boston Celtics of the 1960s were built around the magnificent defensive genius of Bill Russell. And before Big Bill there had been the breath-taking backcourt combination of Bob Cousy and Bill Sharman, who spearheaded the Celtics' yearly drive to a league title. The 1966-67 Philadelphia 76ers took it all because Wilt Chamberlain scored, passed off, rebounded and played defense, dominating the opposition almost by himself. And George Mikan—"Mister Basketball" himself—was the key to the league dominance enjoyed by the old Minneapolis Lakers.

But the New York Knickerbockers of 1969-70 had no such superstar. Willis Reed was strong off the boards in the fight for rebounds, and he could be relied upon to score in double figures. Walt Frazier was a dazzling playmaker and a marvel on defense. But either Reed or Frazier could be on the bench and the team would win. In place of a superstar, the Knicks had a perfectly balanced team. And they had a coach, William "Red" Holzman, who knew how to blend the talents of his squad into a smooth-running machine no matter which five players were on the floor.

What were they like, those first eight players? What did they have that made them so perfect for a team that relied on teamwork? They did not come together by accident. Red Holzman and his associates had carefully scouted and picked them in the college drafts, or in trades with other NBA teams. Holzman knew what he wanted—a team that could play his style of basketball—and he systematically went about putting it together. This is what he saw when he looked over his New York team at the beginning of the 1969–70 season.

Willis Reed. A 1964 graduate of Grambling (Louisiana) College, the 6'9" strongman joined the Knicks for the 1964–65 season and averaged 19.5 points per game and snared 1175 rebounds as center. He was voted Rookie of the Year and it looked as if New York finally had the center it had been hunting for so long. Then, before the next season got under way, the Knicks picked up 6'10½" Walt Bellamy in a trade with the Baltimore Bullets. Reed—the All-Star freshman center—was converted to a sophomore forward.

Reed had to readjust his thinking and playing style, both offensively and defensively. His scoring average declined and many observers thought the Knicks had made a wrong move. "If I had my choice," said an opposing coach, "I'd take him over all the other forwards in this league—but then I'd play him at center."

By the end of the 1966–67 season Reed had adjusted to his new position and was again averaging 20 points per game and playing a major role as a rebounder. In 1967–68 he continued to shine. Then, halfway through the 1968–69 schedule, Bellamy was traded to Detroit, in exchange for forward Dave DeBusschere. Suddenly Reed had his old position at center and he proceeded to turn in his finest season, averaging 21 points per game and grabbing 1191 rebounds. He was ready for the championship season.

Walt Frazier. At 6'4" and 200 pounds, Frazier was famous for his ball-handling wizardry. In college he had led the Southern Illinois Salukis to a 20–2 record in his junior year and then to first place in the National Invitation Tournament.

He was hand-picked by Eddie Donovan, then the Knicks' general manager, in the first round of the 1967 college draft. "While we like Jimmy Walker of Providence and Earl Monroe of Win-

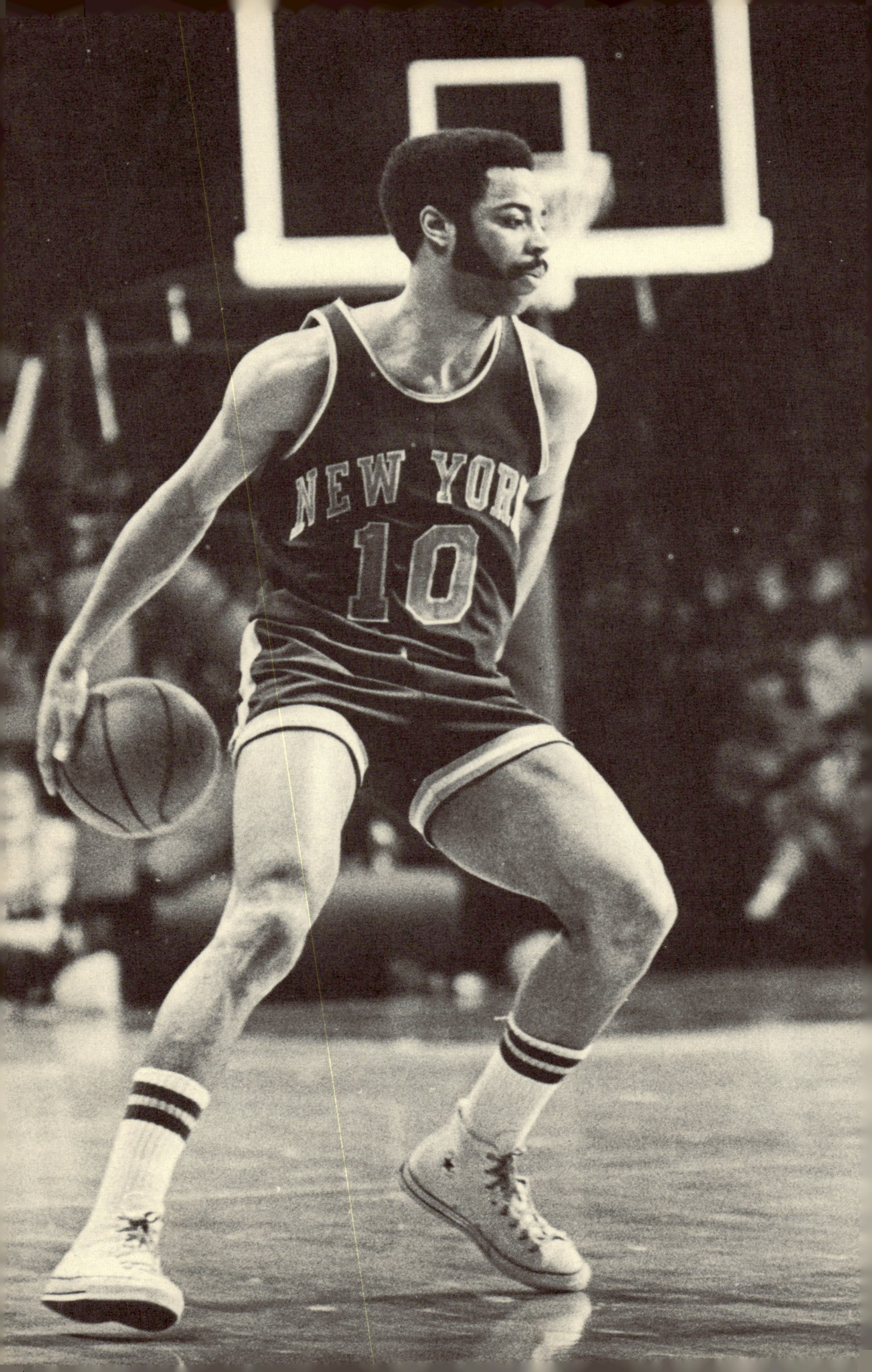
NEW YORK
10

NEW YORK KNICKS, 1969–70

ston-Salem as scorers," Donovan said after the college draft was over, "we really were more impressed with Frazier's overall game. He handled the ball well, had a great sense of direction, and was ahead of the other two on defense. And Southern Illinois used Walt at both guard and forward. Most forwards are good with the ball only if the shot is waiting for them; otherwise they can't think of anything else to do except throw it back to one of the guards. Frazier was different. We felt this boy had to be unusual."

Walt sharpened his basketball tools to a razor-fine edge in the two seasons preceding the 1969–70 campaign. In 1968–69, he scored 17.5 points per game, but he really made his mark with his defensive play. The league coaches voted Walt top place on the official All-Defensive team. At 24, he was the youngest player on the squad, but won 25 out of 28 possible votes.

Dave DeBusschere. There was something lacking in the Knicks' game through the first half of the 1968–69 season. They won only six of their first 19 games. By mid-December their record was 18–17, but it was clear they were not going anywhere fast. Then, on December 19, Walt Bellamy and

Walt Frazier was the Knicks' playmaker and best ball-handler.

Howard Komives were traded to the Detroit Pistons for Dave DeBusschere. The New York club exploded. They strung together 10- and 11-game win streaks and finished strong. In the playoffs, they defeated the strong Baltimore Bullets and barely missed upsetting the Bill Russell-led Celtics for the Eastern Division championship.

There was no doubt that DeBusschere was the difference between the so-so Knicks of the beginning of the year and the hot team after December. Kevin Loughery of the Baltimore Bullets commented that DeBusschere helped the Knicks in four positions, not just one. First, he was the best forward they had ever had. Second, they were able to move Reed from forward to center, where he was nothing short of tremendous. Third, Bill Bradley, who wasn't quick enough for the backcourt, was shifted to forward, where he was great. Finally, the shake-up made it possible for Walt Frazier to play all the time at guard rather than trading off with Bradley.

Bill Bradley. The sharp-eyed, determined Bradley was nicknamed "Mr. President" by teammates who admired his ambition both in basketball and beyond it. After a phenomenal career as

Dave DeBusschere, the Knicks' rugged forward, goes up for a shot.

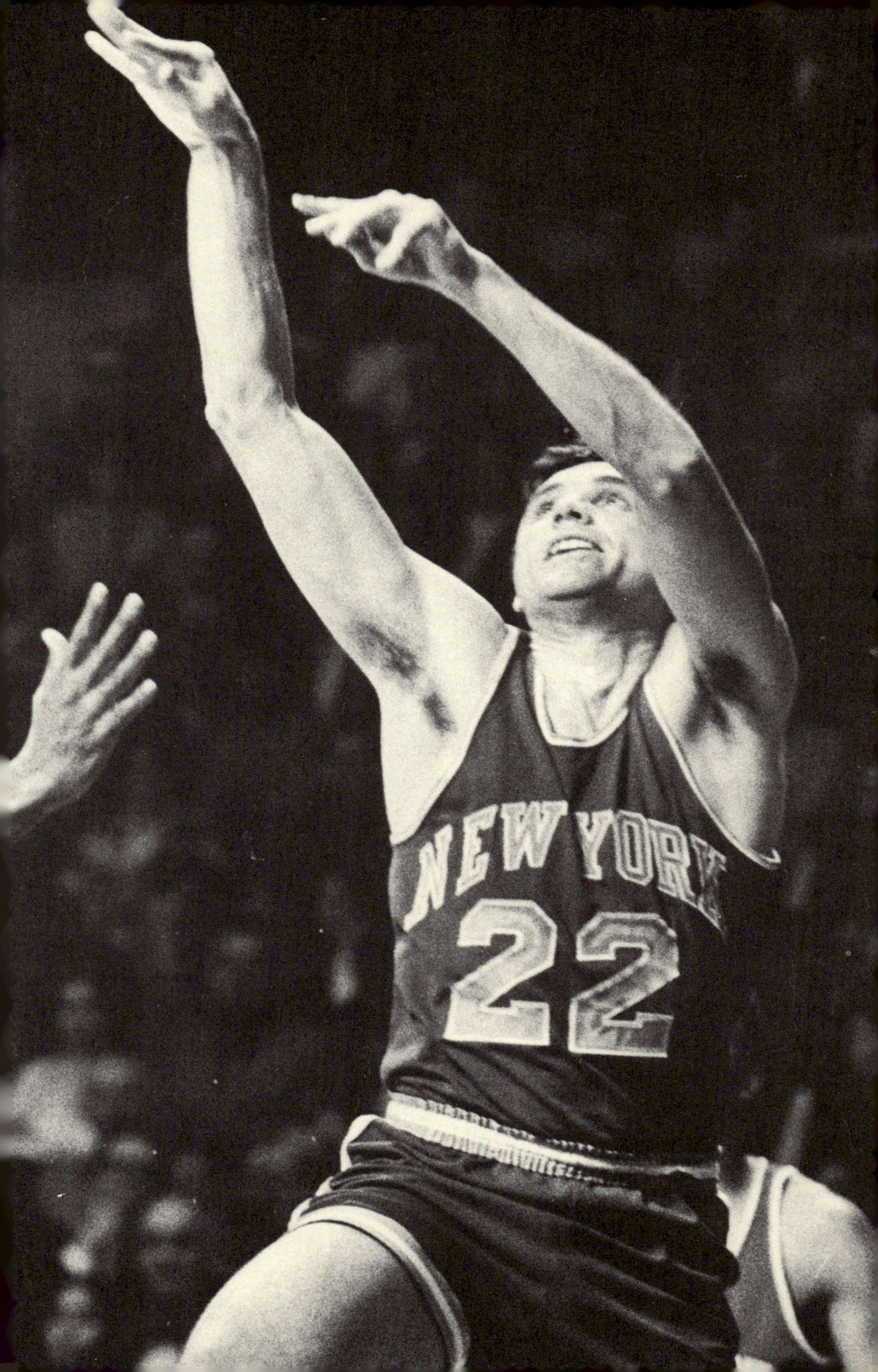
NEW YORK
22

a Princeton All-American, Bradley was a first draft choice by the Knicks in 1965. But he also won a Rhodes scholarship and chose to study at England's Oxford University rather than play for the Knicks for a high bonus. But when he completed his studies, Bradley joined the Knicks during 1967-68 because he wanted to see just how well he could do against the world's best basketball players.

Cazzie Russell. Another first draft choice, in 1966, was Michigan All-American Cazzie Russell. At 6'5½" and 220 pounds, Cazzie was a half-inch taller and 15 pounds heavier than Bradley, but Bradley's superior defensive play and passing gave him a slight edge when the starting five were chosen. Cazzie was good enough to make just about any other team's starting five, but for the Knicks he shuttled in and out of games and added a lightning punch to the Knick attack.

Dick Barnett. Starting at the other guard position along with Frazier was 33-year-old Dick Barnett. After graduating from Tennessee A&I in 1959, Barnett bounced around the pros until he finally settled with the Knicks in 1965. He soon became an integral part of the team, a player whose experience, defensive skills and steady outside shooting helped make New York a smooth-moving machine.

NEW YORK KNICKS, 1969–70

Mike Riordan. Riordan was a hustling player who doggedly worked to prove he could make the team. A star at Providence College, Mike graduated in 1967 but couldn't catch on with an NBA team. He spent the 1967–68 season playing in the Eastern League and signed with the Knicks as a free agent in 1968. And in the 1968–69 season he had exhibited the desire and the ability to be a reliable addition to the team.

Dave Stallworth. Dave had been the Knicks other first-round draft choice (along with Bill Bradley) in 1965. But soon afterward it was discovered that Stalls had a heart condition. It appeared that he would never be able to play basketball again. He retired from the game on the advice of doctors. But by 1969, Stallworth's condition had disappeared. He made his comeback as one of Holzman's top substitutes at forward, when the Knicks went gunning for the 1970 title.

In addition to the top eight, the Knicks had Nate Bowman, a 6'10", 230-pound center who could relieve Reed when he needed a rest or got into foul trouble. Completing the team roster, but destined to see little action, were sophomores Don May and Bill Hosket, and rookie John Warren.

In the opening game of the 1969–70 season, the Knicks faced the Seattle Supersonics at Madison Square Garden. The Supersonics were a notch below the really strong teams in the league. But their star player-coach, Lennie Wilkens, one of the top backcourt players in the NBA, was really "up" for the game. He was expected to give Walt Frazier a difficult time in their first encounter of the season.

The starting Knick five—Reed, Bradley, De-Busschere, Barnett and Frazier—kicked things off with an awesome display of slick, quick offense. One play was typical of their offensive style. Barnett flipped the ball into play and Frazier dribbled it into Seattle territory. As Wilkens came to meet him, Walt bounced the ball to Bill Bradley, who began dribbling and edging toward the basket. Willis Reed moved toward Bradley and it looked as if Reed was trying to gain position between Bradley and the basket, giving Bill a screen over which he could shoot. Frazier, in the meantime, maneuvered closer to Bradley, bringing Wilkens with him. To Wilkens, it seemed clear that Bradley was going to shoot, so he dropped off Frazier for a moment to try to bother Bradley.

That was the defensive lapse the Knicks had planned on. Walt suddenly turned on his speed, darting past Wilkens and meeting Bradley's pass

Frazier takes a risk, reaching around Jerry West trying to steal the ball.

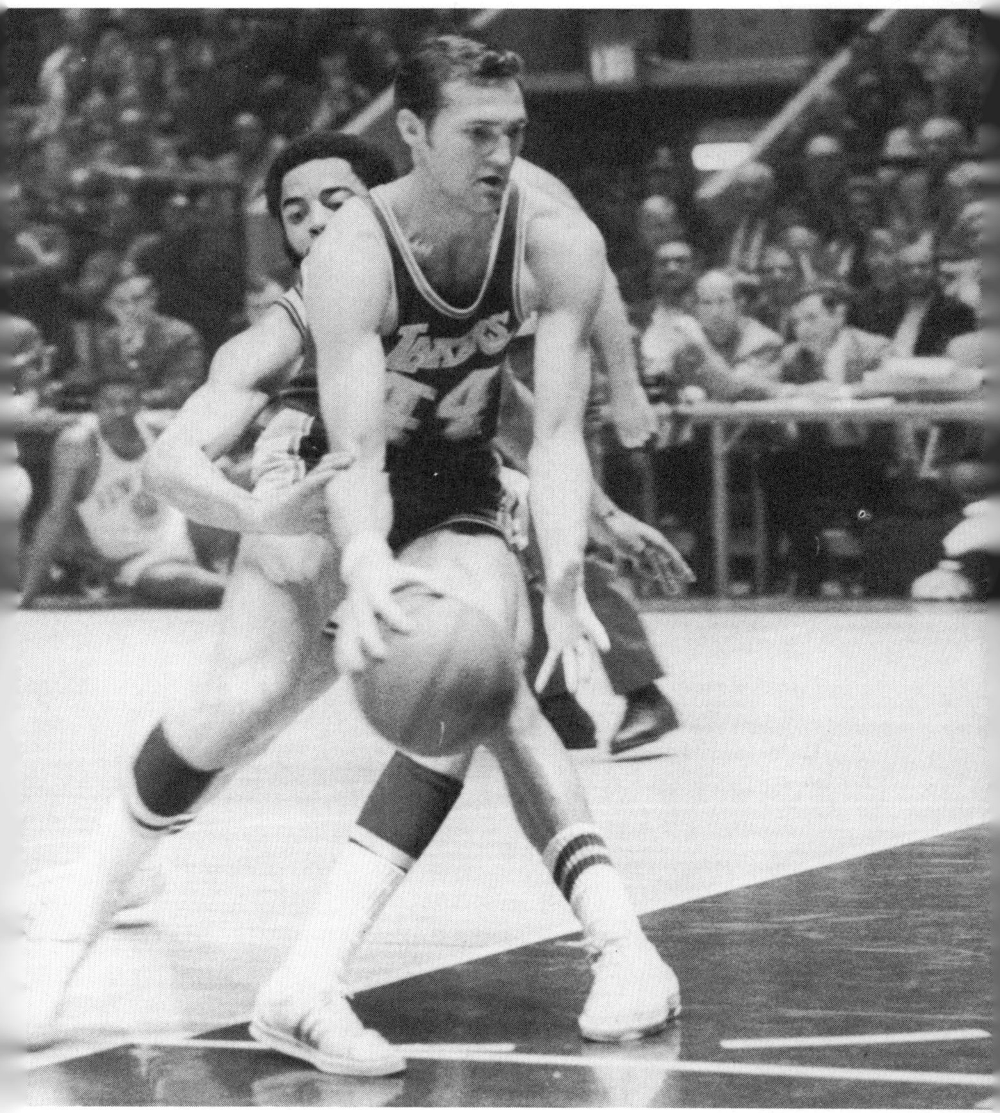

on his way to the basket. A split-second later Frazier was in the air, dropping in an uncontested two-pointer.

The Knicks were communicating with each other; they had timing, speed, alertness and assurance. As Bradley said later in the season, "When we're right, we are like a finely attuned machine, no stars, no selfishness. It's fun just to watch a great player like Frazier," he continued, "but as a team it's also fun, because when one of us moves, the other four adjust. Everybody's moving, taking part in every play. The joy of it comes from playing this game the way it should be played."

That Seattle contest also featured much of the finely developed Knickerbocker defense. After a Knick score, for instance, the New Yorkers backpedaled on defense, picking up their opponents. Walt Frazier did more than "pick up his man." Frazier covered Wilkens like a cat stalking a mouse. If Lenny got the ball, Walt was on him, reading his moves, keeping him off-balance, trying to press him into making a bad pass. Often Frazier's lightning-fast hands would move suddenly for the ball, knocking it away from an opponent in the middle of a dribble. He gambled each time he tried for the steal because if he missed, his man would be uncovered. Yet gambling, too, was part of the defensive plan. Bill Bradley explained,

NEW YORK KNICKS, 1969–70

"When Walt gambles on defense to make a steal, I have to take his man if he misses. If I don't, Walt looks bad, and if that happened often, he would lose confidence that I am there behind him. Eventually, he would stop gambling, and with that, our whole defense would fall apart."

Frazier particularly liked to get a psychological advantage on his opponent. "I wait for a guy to get careless," he said. "Like on a pass-in, when a guy is mad because his man has just scored. Then if I steal off him, he'll tend to tighten up and then you can really put the pressure on him. Say the guy I'm guarding is a good outside shooter. Then I try to force him to drive on me rather than let him set up for a shot. And if he is a good lay-up man, then I try to make him take the outside shot."

With Frazier doing his job, particularly on Lenny Wilkens, and the rest of the Knicks doing theirs, Seattle didn't stand a chance in that first game. The Knicks clobbered the Sonics 126–101.

Winning soon became a way of life for Holzman's squad. They took 26 of their first 28 games, including a record-setting 18 straight. The 18th win of the streak was a breath-taking victory over the Cincinnati Royals. With 16 seconds left in the game the Knicks trailed 105–100. Willis Reed had been fouled and he sank both shots. 105–102.

Then a Royal, under fierce defensive pressure, was called for traveling. Dave DeBusschere grabbed the inbounds pass at midcourt, and drove in for a lay-up. 105–104.

The Royals needed only to hold on to the ball for a few seconds to win. But the Knicks were pressing and Reed batted away a pass as a Royal was reaching for it. Frazier recovered the ball and streaked downcourt. He shot, probably the last shot of the game, and missed. But he was fouled in the act of shooting. With two seconds left on the clock, he had two shots coming. Looking as cool as any boy practicing free throws in his backyard, Walt sank the first, tying the score. Still appearing relaxed, he shot again and made it, giving the Knicks a 106–105 victory and their 18th win in a row.

The pressure of keeping up the winning streak placed enormous strain on the entire squad. After their heroics against Cincinnati, the Knicks played an uncommonly sloppy game against the mediocre Detroit Pistons and went down to defeat. They had set the record and outrun the rest of the league. Now it appeared they needed time out to relax. Playing far below their standard of excellence, the New Yorkers faltered, losing four of their next seven contests.

The Knicks returned to their winning ways

soon enough, however, and slumped only once—when toward the end of the regular schedule the regulars needed rest and Holzman varied his lineup from game to game. Even then the Knicks won more than they lost, and the substitutes acquired more confidence in themselves. With the exhausting playoffs still to come, it was important for the starting five to relax a bit.

One player who took little time off and even seemed restless when he wasn't playing was Willis Reed. He took his responsibilities as center and captain of the Knicks so seriously that he insisted on playing even when he was sick or injured.

Willis faced some of the greatest challenges in the game. Night after night he came up against such basketball giants as Lew Alcindor, Wes Unseld and Wilt Chamberlain. Willis had to score against them and stop them on defense or the Knicks would lose. Another big challenger was Connie Hawkins, of the Phoenix Suns. Connie had been the best player in the American Basketball Association and had signed to play in the NBA for the 1969–70 season. A high scorer with a fantastic arsenal of offensive moves, he challenged Reed directly one night in February of 1970. Although Hawkins usually played forward, his coach had moved him to center opposite Reed, thinking that "the challenge of playing Reed

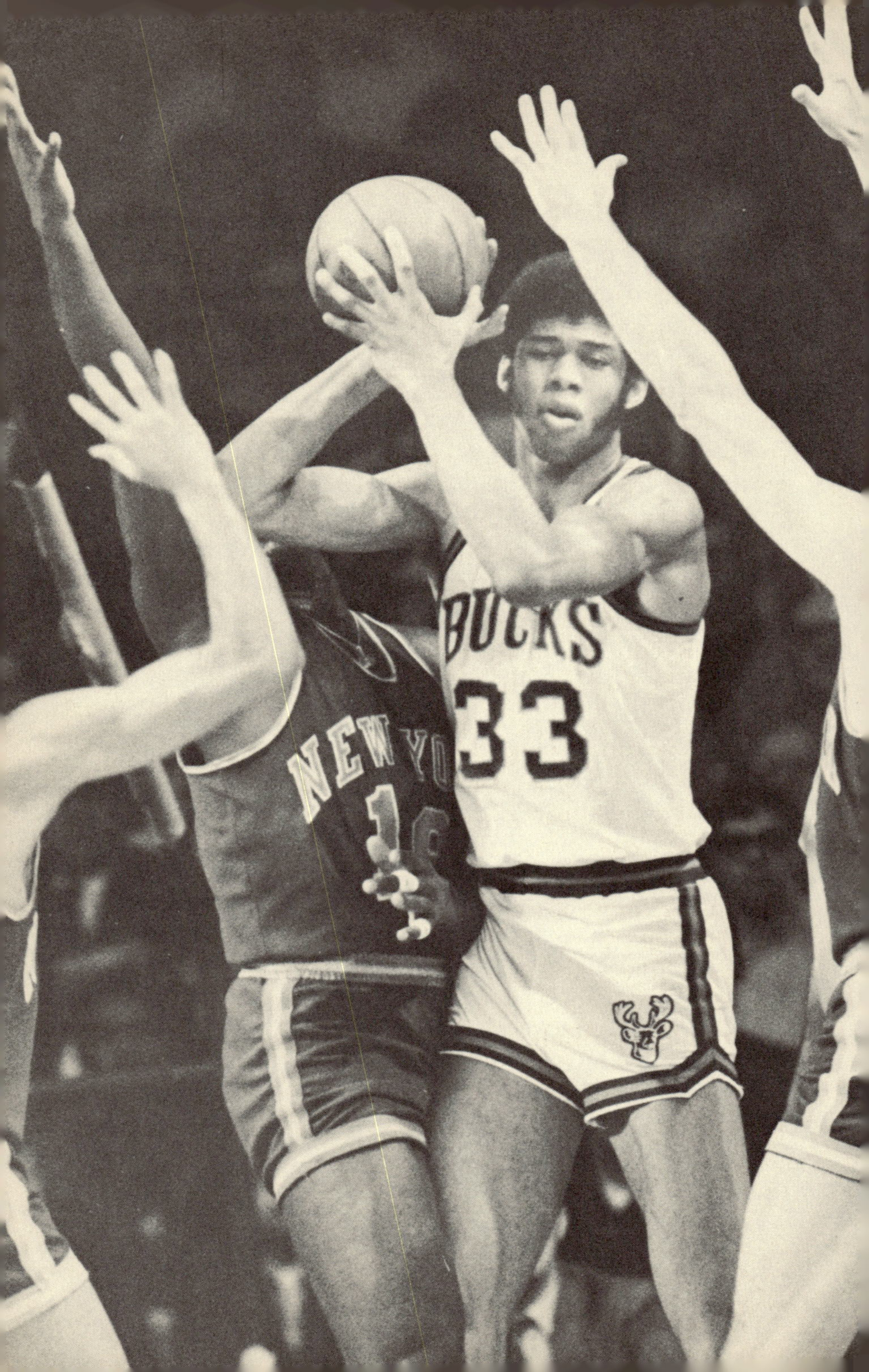
BUCKS
33
NEW YO

might bring out the best in Hawkins."

Reed rose to the occasion. On the very first play of the game, Willis took a pass from Frazier and started maneuvering in the pivot. Hawkins matched Willis move for move for a few moments. Then, all at once, Willis put together a series of moves and fakes, and left Hawkins behind and went up to score.

"I knew it was coming," Hawkins said after the game, "but I couldn't do anything about it."

Red Auerbach, general manager of the Boston Celtics, met general agreement when he said, "Willis Reed is the best center in basketball right now. He's the best on offense and the best on defense."

The regular season ended with the Knicks on top in the Eastern Division. They had won 60 games and lost only 22, for a .732 percentage. Milwaukee was four games behind in the standings. They had come on strong in the final weeks, prompting some observers to speculate that the Knicks might have big trouble if they met Milwaukee in the playoffs.

First the New Yorkers had to take on the third-place Baltimore Bullets. The Bullets wanted re-

Lew Alcindor of the Milwaukee Bucks finds himself hemmed in by the Knick defense.

venge for their humiliation the previous year. Baltimore had finished first in the Division and met the Knicks in the first round of the playoffs. The underdog Knicks had drubbed them in four straight games. In 1970 the Bullets hoped to turn the tables.

The first game of their best-of-seven series was played at Madison Square Garden. Baltimore's biggest guns were Earl (The Pearl) Monroe, whose sharpshooting accounted for 39 points, and a reserve guard named Fred Carter, who contributed 21. In addition, Wes Unseld snared 31 rebounds, to go with 14 points scored. For the Knicks, the heroes included Reed with 21 rebounds and 30 points, DeBusschere with 22 points and Bradley with 21.

At the end of regulation time, the score was tied. In overtime play the Knicks found a new hero as Walt Frazier stole the ball from the Bullets four times. The game ended after the second overtime period with the Knicks in front 120–117. After the game, Frazier modestly explained his game-winning steals: "I've just got to be lucky, and I was."

For the next six games coach Holzman and his team concentrated even harder on defense. The second contest, played on Baltimore's home court, saw the Knicks hold the Bullets to 99 points while scoring 106. Then Baltimore came fighting back. They notched their first win of the playoffs by defeating New York 127–113, then evened the series at two wins apiece by taking the Knicks 102–92. Monroe and Carter continued to score, Gus Johnson chipped in with points and rebounds—but it was Wes Unseld's rebounding that threatened to end the Knicks' championship hopes in the first round of the playoffs.

New York rallied in the fifth game and topped the Bullets, 101–80. Then Baltimore came back with a 96–87 win. Thus everything depended on game number 7. With 19,500 New York fans cheering them on, the Knicks battered the Bullets, 127–114.

The Knicks had stood up to the playoff pressure, playing their game and winning. Walt Frazier once described what was needed: "It's the man who wants to handle the ball in every clutch situation that you really need; the guy who wants to take the key shot, or go for the key steal. He's the one who will win a playoff for you. The guy who comes up with ten baskets in the last quarter of a regular season game when his team is leading or trailing by 30 points is probably not going to be all that great when the pressure is hard."

Next up for the Knicks were the Milwaukee Bucks. They had just trounced the Philadelphia

76ers four games to one in their opening round. The Bucks' Lew Alcindor, with some shooting help from Flynn Robinson and Bob Dandridge, had stopped the well-balanced 76ers. An indication of how strong the Bucks could be was their second win over Philadelphia—by a score of 156–120.

So the men of Red Holzman went to work. Walt Frazier was assigned to guard Flynn Robinson and did everything but put handcuffs on him. Although he had averaged 22 points a game, Robinson had weak points and Frazier went after them. "Flynn likes to spin back to the middle, but he has trouble dribbling to his left," he explained. Time and again he forced Robinson to the right side of the court so that Robinson would have to move to his left. The result was that Robinson didn't score a point in the first half of the first game as New York won 110–102. Robinson wasn't in the line-up for the last 18 minutes of the second game, a tight 112–111 New York triumph. After that he rode the bench through most of the series.

Still, the Knicks had to get around Lew Alcindor. To do this, they adopted a new strategy on

Coming off the bench, Cazzie Russell gets off a shot against Lew Alcindor.

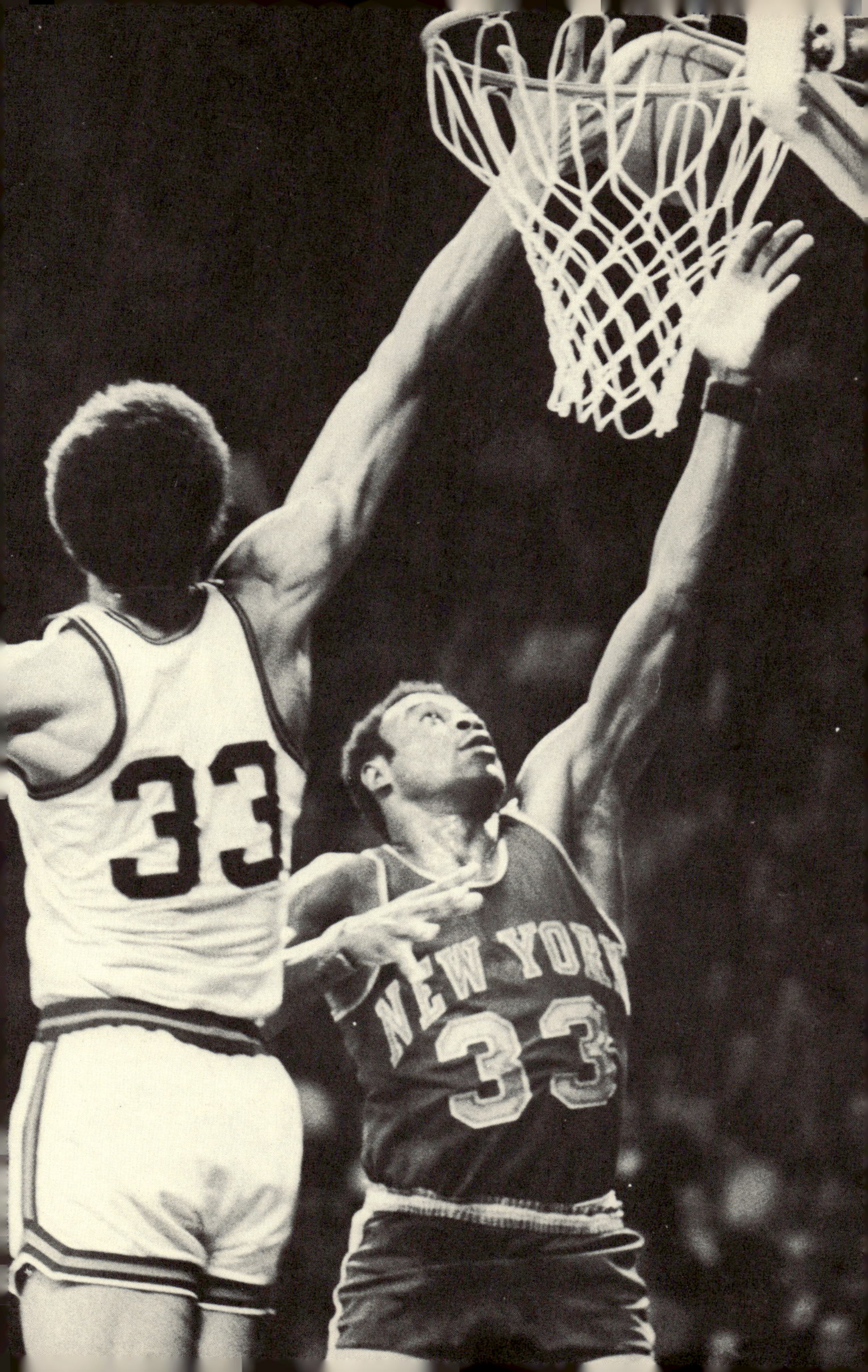
33
NEW YORK
33

offense. Instead of fighting Alcindor under the boards, Reed stayed away from the basket. Since Reed was a great outside shooter, Alcindor was forced to come out and guard him. This put Lew out of rebounding and blocking position. Since the middle was open, Dave DeBusschere played an important rebounding role, picking up 16 in the first game. Even "little" Walt Frazier grabbed 12 rebounds in the second contest.

Milwaukee came back after the first two losses to win the third game 101–96, but this victory was their dying gasp. New York wrapped up the series with consecutive victories of 117–105 and 132–96. The most crushing weapon the Knicks had was Reed's outside shooting. His deceptive moves and accurate eye were just too much for Alcindor.

So far the Knicks were running true to form. The starting five were outshooting, outdefending and wearing down their opponents. And the substitutes—Russell, Riordan, Stallworth and Bowman—were playing so well that the starters could rest without weakening the Knicks' game in the least.

As Eastern Division champs, the Knicks now faced the toughest hurdle of all, the Los Angeles Lakers. Both teams had good reason to want a victory: neither had ever won an NBA championship. The Lakers had a team that boasted three

NEW YORK KNICKS, 1969-70

all-time greats. Heading the list was Wilt Chamberlain, formerly the hero of the great Philadelphia 76ers who had toppled the Boston Celtics from the championship in 1967. The huge center, who held many of the all-time NBA scoring records, had seriously injured his leg early in the 1969-70 season. It appeared for awhile that his career might be over and it seemed certain that he would be out for the whole year. But as the playoffs drew near, Wilt began working out again. By the time of the championship series, he was a major threat to the Knicks.

Laker forward Elgin Baylor had been chosen as a starter on the All-Time NBA team. After season upon season of basketball warfare, he was no longer young but he still had many of his legendary skills. He had never been on a champion team and this was perhaps his last chance to contribute to that achievement.

The third Laker superstar was guard Jerry West. An admirable playmaker and a fantastic scorer, West had won the league's scoring title for 1970. He was also famous as a competitor who only got better as the going got worse.

Along with these dominant three, the Lakers also fielded rookie Dick Garrett, a strong defensive player and good shooter, and Keith Erickson, a clever feeder and reliable scorer. The Laker substitutes couldn't match the Knick bench, although such men as seven-foot Mel Counts and veteran John Tresvant were ready and able to do their share when called upon.

The series opened in New York on Friday, April 24, 1970. In October of 1969, the New York Mets had won baseball's World Championship. Now another title was within reach and New Yorkers had basketball fever. On subway trains, in offices, in classrooms, in homes there were fevered debates about the Knicks' chances of taking the title. Could the home team overcome Chamberlain, Baylor and West?

The fans got their answer in the first game. Outweighed by 50 pounds and shorter by five inches, Willis Reed fought Wilt Chamberlain for every rebound and harassed him every time he had the ball. When the Knicks had the ball, Reed used the same strategy he had employed so successfully against Lew Alcindor, staging an eye-popping display of outside shooting that rang up a total of 37 points for the game. Big Wilt scored only 17.

In the meantime, Walt Frazier hounded Jerry West on defense, seeming to anticipate the Laker guard's every move. On offense, Frazier was at his delightful best, setting up plays, feeding Bill Bradley and Reed, driving for the basket.

NEW YORK KNICKS, 1969–70

The Knicks built an early lead and the Lakers were forced to play catch-up basketball from the first moments. Jerry West scored 33 points, and Baylor sank 21. But the Knicks had the upper hand. Led by Reed's 37 points, the Knicks won 124–112.

But the Lakers hadn't come to New York to be swept off the court. The second game was a thriller, bringing out the hand-clapping, foot-stomping emotions of the basketball fans. At the end of the first half the teams were tied 52–52. At the three-quarter mark it was still knotted 81–81. West's outside gunning was matching Reed's hot shooting. Chamberlain was leaning heavier on Reed, using his great strength, and getting better position under the boards for rebounds and baskets. With 46 seconds left on the game clock, the score was 103 apiece. Then West was fouled in the act of shooting and stepped to the line for two free shots. With the crowd suddenly hushed, he coolly sank both. The Knicks couldn't score and West's shots gave the Lakers a 105–103 victory. West scored 34 points, followed by Chamberlain with 19 points and Dick Garrett with 17. The leading scorers for the losing Knicks were Reed with 29, Barnett with 19 and DeBusschere with 18.

Now the scene shifted cross-country for the next two games at the Forum in Los Angeles. Here the

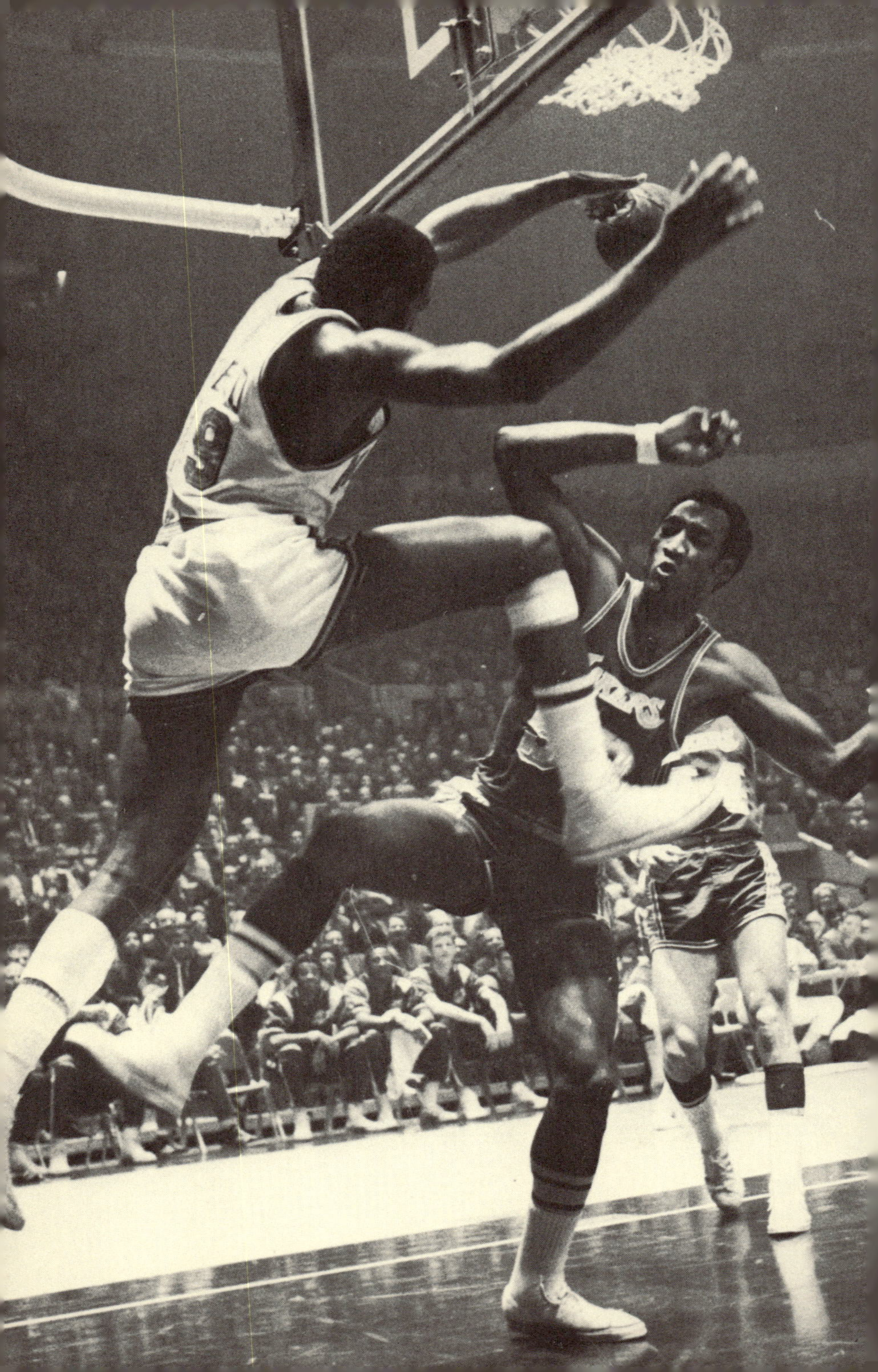

NEW YORK KNICKS, 1969-70

Lakers had a dedicated crowd rooting them on. The New Yorkers needed to win at least one of the two games in Los Angeles or they would return to Madison Square Garden behind three games to one.

The third game was as rough and as close as the second one. Frazier continued to dog West and the Chamberlain-Reed struggle continued. The Knick shooting was sharp, the defense was strong, and the play was crisp. Bill Bradley really hit his stride, leading DeBusschere perfectly with his passes as Dave barrelled in for baskets.

With two seconds left, the Knicks scored to go ahead by two. The Lakers' inbounds pass went to Jerry West who made a long desperation toss at the basket. To the surprise of everyone and to the joy of the Laker fans, the ball swished through the net. The 55-foot shot tied the game and sent it into overtime. But the Knicks recovered quickly from the shock and outplayed Los Angeles in the overtime, winning 111-108.

The fourth game found the Lakers charging back behind the performance of Jerry West, who scored 37 points and made 18 assists. Again the game went into overtime, but this time West was

Willis Reed seems about to hit his head on the backboard as he goes up for a rebound.

the hero and put the Lakers ahead to stay. The final score: Los Angeles 121, New York 115. Baylor and Chamberlain backed West's efforts with impressive games of their own. Elgin notched 30 points and Wilt netted 18 points and snared 25 rebounds. Barnett was high man for the Knicks with 29.

The Knicks came home to Madison Square Garden with the series tied 2–2 and the home-court edge on their side. The fans cheered wildly when the Knicks took the floor—it seemed that New York could win the championship in the next two games. Then tragedy struck.

The Lakers spurted to a 25–15 lead with a little less than four minutes left in the first quarter. Then Reed, on a drive toward the basket, twisted the wrong way and slammed to the floor, writhing in pain. Reed was helped off to the dressing room and Knick hopes were in shambles. Word came back from the dressing room that Willis had severely strained two thigh muscles and wouldn't appear for the rest of the game.

Without Reed, New York's chances of conquering the Lakers seemed to be next to nothing. Who would handle Chamberlain? Bowman was tall

Tragedy strikes the Knicks in the fifth game against the Lakers. Willis Reed writhes in pain after injuring his right leg.

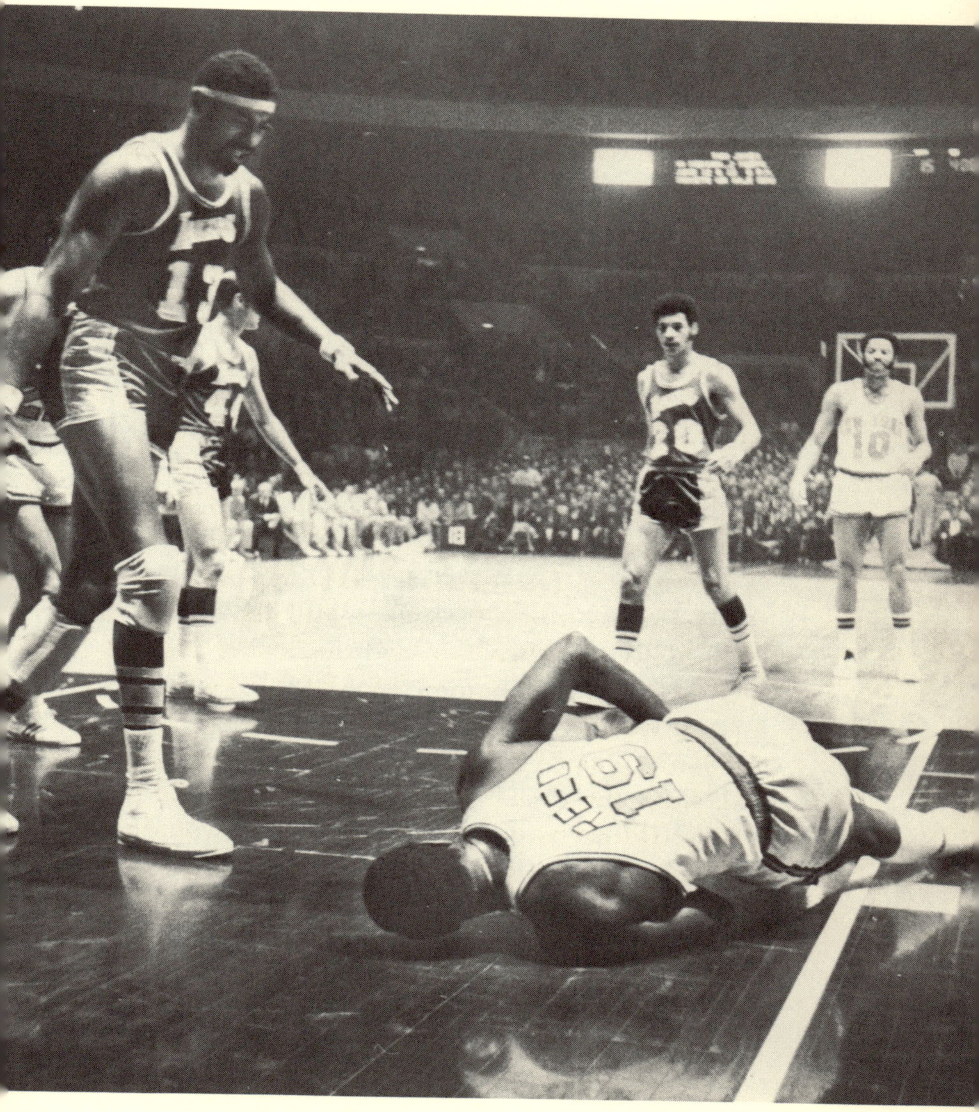
REED
19

enough but he didn't have the experience; Hosket had even less playing time and seasoning. And there certainly was no substitute who could score the way Willis could. The team might as well give up.

In the next three quarters the Knicks outran, outmaneuvered, outdefensed and totally outplayed a "superior" Laker team. So determined was the Reed-less Knick defense that the Lakers gave up the ball without shooting 30 times—on bad passes, calls for traveling, or outright Knick steals. Ten of those turnovers came in the last quarter, when possession of the ball was most crucial. Whenever Chamberlain had the ball, he was double-teamed, sometimes triple-teamed, by Bowman, Hosket and DeBusschere or Stallworth. When West had it, he found Frazier, Bradley, Russell, Riordan or Barnett collapsing on him, sometimes two at a time, sometimes three.

The tenacious defensive ring around Chamberlain so throttled him that he managed to score only four points in the second half. And Jerry West—the supreme clutch-player—was completely shut out from the field in the second half.

Meanwhile, the Knicks were scoring. At the final buzzer the score was: Knicks 107, Lakers 100. New York had made one of the great comebacks in basketball history.

NEW YORK KNICKS, 1969-70

The next day it was announced that Reed would not play in the sixth game. When the game got under way back in Los Angeles, it was clear the Laker game plan had been changed to meet the new circumstances.

The Knicks did their best, but it seemed as if they had used themselves up in the tremendous New York comeback. The Lakers, embarrassed by their poor showing in New York, were eager for revenge. As Reed watched unhappily from the bench, the Knicks were routed 135-113. Chamberlain went on a scoring spree, hitting for 45 points. West scored 33 and New York was never in contention.

The teams came back to New York for the seventh and deciding game of the series. No one knew for sure if Willis Reed would play. If he did play, he might not be able to help the Knicks. New York fans were gloomy.

On the night of the game, the Knicks came out to warm up without Reed. As the minutes ticked by, spectators began to doubt he would appear. Then shortly before time for the opening tap-off Reed appeared and began to make his way to the floor. The crowd broke into a thunderous roar at Reed's appearance and the sound seemed to build even higher as he flipped a few practice shots into the nets. Chamberlain and the Lakers stood nearby, measuring the man and wondering how much he had recovered.

The ball went up for the jump and the game was on. The Knicks gained possession and seconds later Captain Reed pumped in a one-hander for two points. Then he shifted to defense. Now crucial questions would be answered. Could he control Chamberlain? Could his leg take the hammering demands of running, jumping and bumping bodies with Big Wilt? Reed was slower than usual, his mobility was undeniably restricted, and he clearly favored the injured leg.

Chamberlain held the physical advantage. But he didn't have the psychological advantage. He had not expected Willis to play, yet there he was, the Knicks' leader, the man whose very presence seemed to inspire them to basketball deeds beyond their individual talents.

Reed worked hard, draining every ounce of mileage out of the leg. It was painful but he managed to control Chamberlain as they fought for points and rebounds. Reed scored only one more basket but while he was in, the Knicks built up a big lead over the Lakers. He came out in the second quarter and did not return, but the rest of the

With Reed out in the seventh and deciding game of the championship series, another Knick substitute, Mike Riordan, does his share by scoring against Chamberlain.

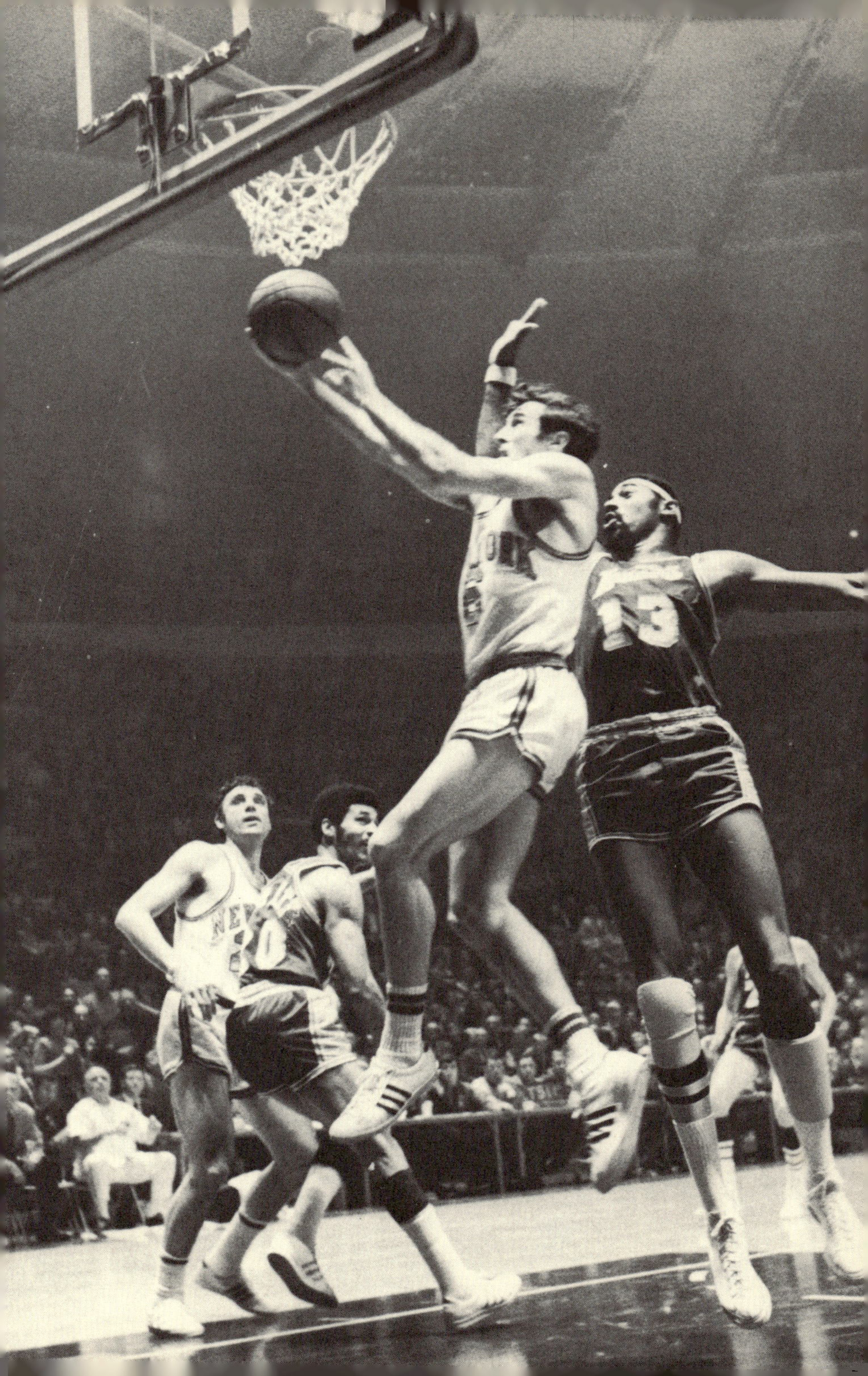

team held on to the lead for dear life.

Frazier seemed to be all over the floor. He was a demon on defense and he took over the responsibility for scoring, racking up 36 points. He also made 19 assists, tying Bob Cousy's all-time playoff record. A doubly bruising DeBusschere assumed the burden of rebounding from Reed and picked 17 off the boards, as well as adding 18 precious points. Also on target were Barnett with 21 points, and Bradley with 17.

Masterminding it all was Red Holzman. He shuttled players in and out of the game, watched for Laker weaknesses and corrected Knick mistakes. When the last buzzer of the season sounded, the scoreboard lights told the story: Knicks 113, Visitors 99.

The papers told the story the next day. But they couldn't express in print and pictures the joy felt by the players and by the fans, the broadcasters and the writers who had followed the team's fortunes for many frustrating years. "We're Number One!" everyone chanted, cheering the Davids who had slain the Goliaths to become champions of the NBA.

New York Knicks, 1969-70

Statistics

Regular season:

Team record: Won 60, lost 22. Finished first in Eastern Division.

Individual leaders:

	Games	Points	Points per Game	Rebounds	Assists
Reed	81	1,755	21.7	1,126	161
Frazier	77	1,609	20.9	465	629
Barnett	82	1,220	14.9	221	298
DeBusschere	79	1,152	14.6	790	194
Bradley	67	971	14.5	239	268

Playoff record:

First round, vs. Baltimore (best 4 out of 7)

NEW YORK	120**	Baltimore	117
NEW YORK	106	Baltimore	99
New York	113	BALTIMORE	127
New York	92	BALTIMORE	102
NEW YORK	101	Baltimore	80
New York	87	BALTIMORE	96
NEW YORK	127	Baltimore	114

Second round, vs. Milwaukee (best 4 out of 7)

NEW YORK	110	Milwaukee	102
NEW YORK	112	Milwaukee	111
New York	96	MILWAUKEE	101
NEW YORK	117	Milwaukee	105
NEW YORK	132	Milwaukee	96

Championship round, vs. Los Angeles (best 4 out of 7)

NEW YORK	124	Los Angeles	112
New York	103	LOS ANGELES	105
NEW YORK	111*	Los Angeles	108
New York	115*	LOS ANGELES	121
NEW YORK	107	Los Angeles	100
New York	113	LOS ANGELES	135
NEW YORK	113	Los Angeles	99

* Overtime game
** Double overtime

Index

Page numbers in italics refer to photographs.

Alcindor, Lew, 115, *116,* 120–122, *121*
Atlanta Hawks, 91
Auerbach, Arnold (Red), 6, 79, 80, 117

Baechtold, Jim, 12
Baltimore Bullets, 12–13, 24, 25, 27, 55, 76, 81, 85, 102, 106, 117–118, 119
Barksdale, Don, 12
Barnes, Jim, 76
Barnett, Dick, 49, 85, 108, 110, 125, 128, 130, 134
Barry, Rick, 45, 54, 56, 59, 60, 63, 64, 66
Baylor, Elgin, 72, 91, 123, 128
Bellamy, Walt, 48, 49, 102, 103, 105
Boryla, Vince, 28, 34

Boston Celtics, 6–9, 17, 26, 27, 45, 54, 55, 58, 59, 101
  1968–69 team, 69–98
  statistics, 97–98
Boston Garden, 85
Bowman, Nate, 109, 122, 128, 130
Bradley, Bill, 85, 106–108, 109, 110, 112, 124, 127, 130, 134
Brannum, Bob, 7
Braun, Carl, 28, 30, 31
Brian, Frank, 16
Bryant, Em, 81, 82

Carter, Fred, 118
Chamberlain, Wilt, *38, 39,* 40, 41, 44, 45, 46, *47,* 48, 49, *50,* 51, 52, 55, 56, *57,* 58, 59, 60, 61, 63, 64, *65,* 66, 72, 91, *92,* 94, 101, 115, 123,

INDEX

124, 125, 127, 128, 130, 131, 132, *133*
Cincinnati Royals, 58, 113–114
Clifton, Nat (Sweetwater), *5*, 20, 28
Cooper, Chuck, 7
Costello, Larry, 44
Counts, Mel, 124
Cousy, Bob, 6–9, 101, 134
Cunningham, Billy, 41, *42*, 43, 46, 48, 52, 58, 63, 76

Dandridge, Bob, 120
DeBusschere, Dave, 85, 103, 105, 106, *107*, 110, 114, 122, 127, 130, 134
Detroit Pistons, 106, 114
Donovan, Eddie, 103

Ellis, Leroy, 81
Embry, Wayne, 72
Erickson, Keith, *70*, 123

Fort Wayne Pistons, 10, 27
Forum (Los Angeles), 93, 125
Frazier, Walt, 85, 101, 103–105, *104*, 110, *111*, 112, 113, 117, 118, 119, 120, 122, 124, 127, 130, 134
Fulks, Joe, 16–17

Gallatin, Harry, 20, *21*, 28
Gambee, Dave, 44
Garrett, Dick, 123, 125
Grambling College (Grambling, Louisiana), 102
Greer, Hal, 41, 46, 49, 52, 55, 56, 58, 60, 61, *62*, 77,
Guokas, Matt, 44, *74–75*

Hamline University (St. Paul, Minn.), 15
Hannum, Alex, 40, 41, 43, 44, 45, 46, 48, 51, 52, *53*, 54, 59, 60
Harrison, Bob, 17, 34
Havlicek, John, 58, 73, 76, *78*, 79, 82, 84, 85, *88–89*, 90, 91, 93, 94, 96
Hawkins, Connie, 115–117
Henriksen, Don, 12
Hetzel, Fred, 59
Hitch, Lew, 10, 28
Holstein, Jim, 28, 30, 31
Holzman, William (Red), 102, 118
Hosket, Bill, 109, 130
Howell, Bailey, *62*, 72, 73, 84, 85

Indianapolis Olympians, 25, 27

138

INDEX

Jackson, Lucious, 43, 51, 61
Johnson, Gus, 55, 119
Johnston, Neil, 16–17, 27
Jones, K. C., 58
Jones, Sam, 58, 71, 72, *74–75*, 76, 81, 82, 85, 93, 94, *95*, 96
Jones, Wally, 44, 61

Kansas, University of, 39, 40
King, Jim, 59
Komives, Howard, 49, 106
Kundla, John, 5, 6, *32–33*

Lapchick, Joe, 22, 23, 27, 28
Los Angeles Lakers, 72, 91–96, 122–134
Loughery, Kevin, 81, 106

Macauley, Ed, 7–9
Madison Square Garden (New York), 20, 86, 109, 118, 127
Marin, Jack, 81
Martin, Slater, 7, 8, *9*, 13, 16, 17, 20, 23, 25, 26, 30, *32–33*
May, Don, 109
McGuire, Al, 28
McGuire, Dick, 7, 20, 28, 30, 31

Melchionni, Bill, 44
Meschery, Tom, 59
Michigan, University of, 108
Mikan, Ed, 17
Mikan, George, *5*, 6, 7, 8, 9, 10–12, 13, 15, 16, 17, 22, 23, 24, 25, 26, 27, 28, *29*, 30, 31, *32–33*, 34, 101
Mikkelsen, Vern, 5, 7, 13, *14*, 15, 16, 21, 25, 27, 31
Milwaukee Bucks, 73, 117, 119–122
Minneapolis (Minn.) Auditorium, 5
Minneapolis Lakers, 101
  1952–53 team, 3–35, *32–33*
  statistics, 36
Monroe, Earl, 81, 103, 118
Mullins, Jeff, 59

Neumann, Paul, 59
New York Knickerbockers, 17–18, 22, 26, 28–34, 48–49, 58, 72, 76, 82, 85–91
  1969–70 team, 99–136
  statistics, 135–136

139

INDEX

Overbrook High School (Philadelphia), 39
Oxford University (England), 108

Philadelphia 76ers, 71, 72, 76, 82, 84, 120
　1966–67 team, 37–68
　statistics, 67–68
Philadelphia Warriors, 16–17, 24, 27
Phillip, Andy, 16
Phoenix Suns, 73
Pollard, Jim, 7, 13, *14*, 15, 17, 23, 25, 27, 30, 31
Princeton University, 108

Ratkovich, George, 12
Reed, Willis, 48, *50*, 85, *100*, 101, 102–103, 110, 113, 114, 115, 117, 122, 124, 125, *126*, 127, 128, *129*, 131, 132, *133*, 134
Riordan, Mike, 109, 122, 130, *133*
Risen, Arnie, 22
Robertson, Oscar, 41, 56, *79*
Robinson, Flynn, 120
Rochester Royals, 17, 22, 24, 25, 26
Russell, Bill, *ii*, *vi*, 54, 56, 58, *65*, *70*, 71, 76, 77, 79, 80, 81, *83*, 84, 85, 90, 91, 93, 94, *95*, 96, 101, 106
Russell, Cazzie, 108, *121*, 122, 130

St. Louis Hawks, 59, 71
San Francisco Warriors, 45, 54, 59–66, 91
Sanders, Tom (Satch), *57*, 58, 72, 73, 76
Saul, Pep, 7, 12, 28
Schayes, Dolph, 41
Schnittker, Dick, 28
Seattle Supersonics, 109–113
Sharman, Bill, 7, 101
Siegfried, Larry, 73, 76, 84, 91
Simmons, Connie, 28, *29*, 30
Skoog, Whitey, 7, 12, 13, *18–19*, 30, 31
Southern Illinois University, 103
Spectrum, The (Philadelphia, Pa.), 46, 61
Stallworth, Dave, 109, 122, 130
Stanford University, 15
Syracuse Nationals, 17, 25, 26

140

INDEX

Tennessee A & I, 108
Thurmond, Nate, *47*, 54, 59, 60, 61
Tresvant, John, 124

Unseld, Wes, 81, 115, 118, 119

Vanderweghe, Ernie, 28, 30, 31

Walker, Chet, 43, 45, 46, 49, 51, 52, 58, 63
Walker, Jimmy, 103
Wanzer, Bobby, 22
Warren, John, 109
West, Jerry, 72, 76, 91, 94, *111*, 123, 124, 125, 127, 128, 130, 131
Wilkens, Lennie, 110, 112, 113

Zaslofsky, Max, 28